TEXAS
ARCHEOLOGICAL SOCIETY®
PRESERVE YOUR HERITAGE

Texas Archeological Society
86th Annual Meeting

October 23-25, 2015

Omni Houston Hotel - Westside

Sponsored by

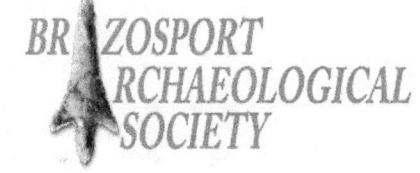

Texas Archeological Society
86ᵗʰ Annual Meeting

Local Arrangements Committee
Brazosport Archeological Society
Fort Bend Archeological Society
Houston Archeological Society (www.txhas.org)

Annual Meeting Organizers: Linda Gorski and Kathleen Hughes
Annual Meeting Registrar: Robert Sewell
Annual Meeting Treasurer: Robert Sewell
Program Co-Chairs: Dr. Jason W. Barrett and Dr. August Costa
Book Exhibit Room: Sandra Rogers
Book Festival: Steve Davis and JTAH
Trans Rio Bravo/Rio Grande International Research Collaboration: Steve Davis and JTAH
Silent Auction Coordinator: Sue Gross
Equiment Wranglers: Larry Golden
Time Keepers: Jay Roussel
Printing and Signage: Tom Williams
Annual Meeting Booklet Publisher: Louis F. Aulbach

Major Sponsor
Silver Eagle Distributors

Supporting Organizations
Atkins Global
Council of Texas Archeologists
Earth Science Rice University
HumanitiesTexas
Journal of Texas Archeology and History
The Summerlee Foundation
Texas Department of Transportation (TxDOT)
Texas Historical Commission
Trader Joe's
VisitHouston!

Texas Archeological Society (www.txarch.org)

Schedule for the 2015 TAS Annual Meeting
Omni Houston Westside

Friday, October 23, 2015

Registration: 8:00AM-5:00PM; Paluxy Foyer
Silent Auction and Exhibits: 8:00AM-5:00PM; Texas Ballroom I, II, III
CTA Meeting: 9:00AM-12:00 noon; Paluxy
Steward's Meeting: 1:00PM-2:00PM; Paluxy
TAS Executive Committee: 2:00PM-2:45PM; Permian
TAS Board Meeting: 2:45PM-3:30PM; Permian
Concurrent Sessions: 2:00PM-6:00PM; Paluxy, Woodbine and Wilcox
Book Festival: 2:00PM-5:00PM; Texas Ballroom Foyer
Public Forum: 7:00PM-8:30PM; Texas Ballroom V, VI, VII
Artifact Identification: 8:30PM-10:00PM; Texas Ballroom V, VI, VII
CTA Careers in Archeology Social: 8:30PM-10:30PM; Texas Ballroom Foyer

Saturday, October 24, 2015

Registration: 8:00AM-12:00 noon; Paluxy Foyer
Silent Auction 8:00AM-4:00PM; Texas Ballroom I, II, III
Exhibit: 8:00AM-5:00PM; Texas Ballroom I, II, III
Book Festival: 8:00-12:00 and 2:00PM-6:00PM; Texas Ballroom Foyer
Concurrent Sessions: 8:00AM-12:00 noon; Paluxy, Permian and Woodbine
1:30PM-6:00PM; Paluxy, Permian and Woodbine
Poster Sessions: 8:00AM-12:00 noon; Texas Ballroom Foyer
2:00PM-3:00PM;Texas Ballroom Foyer
Luncheon and Business Meeting: 12:00PM-1:30PM; Texas Ballroom V, VI, VII
Presidential Reception: 5:00PM-6:00PM; Texas Ballroom Foyer
Cash Bar: 5:00PM-10:00PM; Texas Ballroom Foyer
Banquet: 7:00PM-10:30PM; Texas Ballroom V, VI, VII

Sunday, October 25, 2015

TAS Executive Committee: 7:30AM-9:00AM; Woodbine
TAS Board Meeting: 9:00AM-10:30AM; Woodbine

Time and Places are Subject to Change

Omni Houston Hotel - Westside Floor Plan

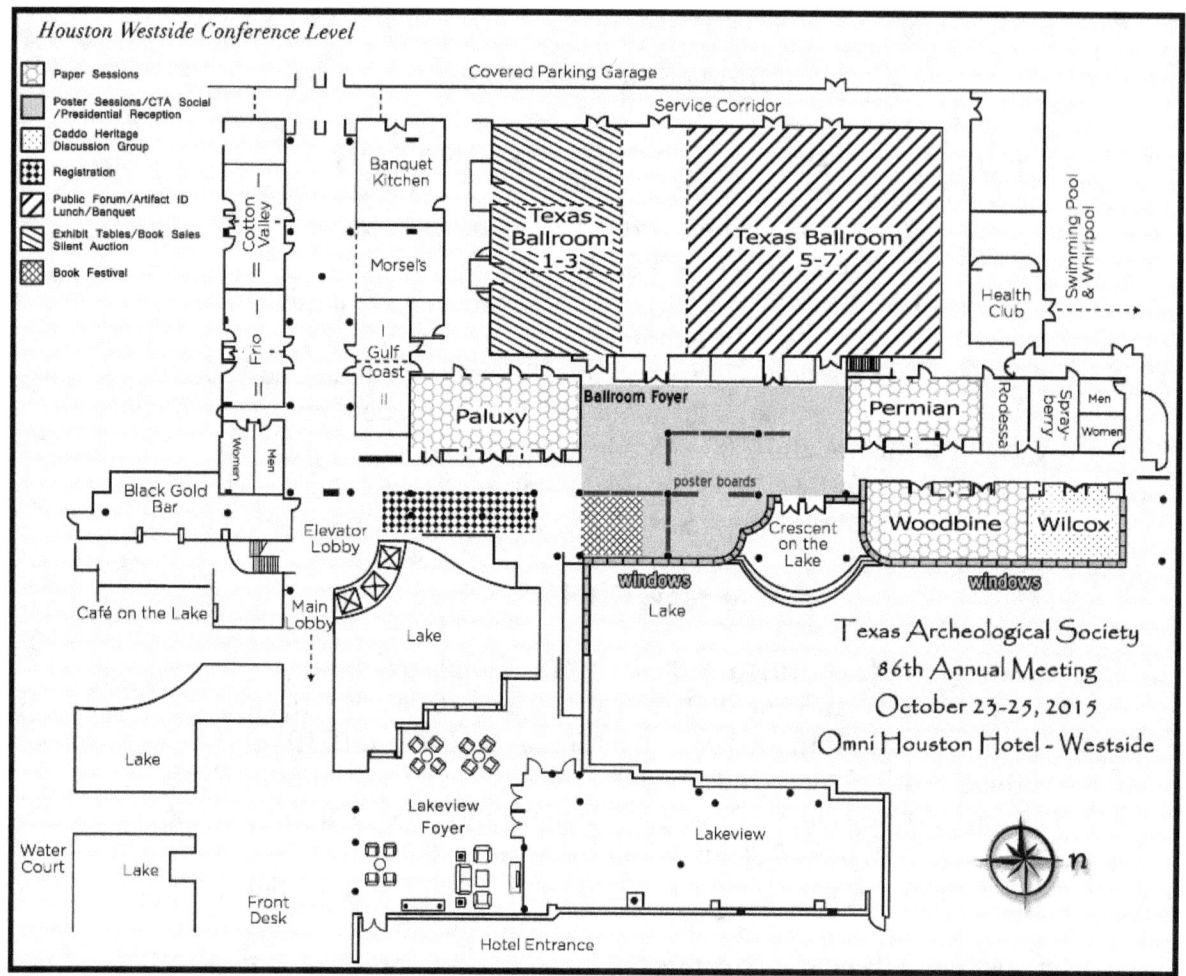

Concurrent Sessions - Friday Afternoon

Paluxy

Symposium: From Burned Rock Features to Battlefields: Current Investigations of the Texas Archeological Stewards Network

2:20 PM **Early Norwegian Settlers on the Texas Frontier: Uncovering the Home of Cleng Peerson** – Rebecca Shelton and Bryan Jameson

2:40 PM **Kemosabe: A New Multi-Component Prehistoric Site Complex Adjacent to the Guadalupe River, Kerr County, Texas** – Steve Stoutamire

3:00 PM **Artifacts from the 1847 Kellum Noble House in Houston Provide a Glimpse of Its Illustrious Past** – Beth Aucoin

3:20 PM **Digging up (and Passing on) Texas History – One Trowel Full at a Time: The Houston Archeological Society's Educational and Public Outreach Programs** – Sharon Menegaz and Linda Gorski

3:40 PM **How a Collection Becomes a TAS Field School** – W. Sue Gross

4:00 PM **Ghosts On the Mudflats: Artifacts from the Lost Townsite of San Jacinto** – Linda Gorski and Larry Golden

4:20 PM BREAK

General Session: Museums and Collections

4:40 PM **The New Witte Museum and Archaeology** – Harry J. Shafer

5:00 PM **The Archaeology of Archaeology** – Maggie McClain

5:20 PM **Disappeared Three Rivers Red-on-Terracotta Bowl** – Robin Gay Wakeland

Concurrent Sessions - Friday Afternoon

Woodbine

General Session: Geo-Spatial Mapping and Remote Sensing

2:00 PM   **A Recalibrated Geoarchaeological Framework of Texas–Revisited** – Ken Lawrence

2:20 PM   **Plugging Away: An Update on TxDOT's Geoarcheological Mapping Program** – James T. Abbott

2:40 PM   **Ground Penetrating Radar Data from an Antelope Creek Site (41PT283) in Potter County, Texas** – Michael Mudd and Robert Z. Selden Jr.

3:00 PM   **Data Collection at 41BX274: Analysis of Remote Sensing Anomalies and the Perez Ranch Jacal** – Jonathan Welch

3:20 PM   **The Use of 3-D GPR As An Aid in the Rediscovery of Spanish Colonial Acequias in San Antonio, Texas** – Kristi Miller Nichols, Laurie M. Steves, Richard A. Sample, and Clint Laffere

3:40 PM   BREAK

Symposium: 3-D Data in Archaeology

4:00 PM   **Beyond the Square Hole: Application of Structure from Motion Photogrammetry to Archaeological Excavation** – Charles W. Koenig, Mark D. Willis, and Steven Black

4:20 PM   **Rapid High Precision Elevation Mapping and Erosion Modeling of a Caddo Mound Site in Henderson County, Texas** – Arlo McKee

4:40 PM   **Using Photogrammetry to Document, Analyze and Reverse-Engineer Grave Markers** – Robert Z. Selden Jr.

5:00 PM   **Everyone Is Doing It: How to Document an Archaeological Site in 3D** – Mark D. Willis

Wilcox

Discussion Group: Discovering Caddo Heritage

3:00 PM -   **TxDOT Roadside Chat with the Caddo Nation of Oklahoma: Discovering**

5:00 PM   **Caddo Heritage** – Laura Cruzada (organizer)

Friday Night Public Forum Speaker

Marilyn Johnson
Room: Texas Ballroom
7:00 PM

Marilyn Johnson, author of *Lives in Ruins: Archaeologists and the Seductive Lure of Human Rubble* is our Public Forum Speaker on Friday night, October 23, 7 p.m. If you have not yet read her book, you'll be able to purchase a copy during her book signing event from 4 – 5 p.m. on Friday at the Second Annual TAS Book Festival sponsored by the JTAH.

Here are a couple of quotes from reviews of her book. As you read these you will note that the words describe all of us at this meeting – professional and avocational alike – who share a passion for archeology!

Lives in Ruins has been praised for demystifying the archeological profession and reporting on it with clarity and humor. The Dallas Morning News wrote: "As archaeologists collect potsherds and spearpoints, Marilyn Johnson became a collector of archaeologists, tracking them to Machu Picchu and to Fishkill, N.Y., to a Caribbean slave plantation and a Philadelphia beer tasting. In Lives in Ruins, she sifts and sorts them, unearthing a treasury of rare characters." Sarah Parcak, K. Kris Hirst, World Archaeology, Discover, and American Archaeologist have recommended it, and Nature called it a "gem of hands-on reportage."

Despite the ominous title of Marilyn Johnson's LIVES IN RUINS: Archaeologists and the Seductive Lure of Human Rubble, this experiential memoir finds life amid the rubble of archaeology. Johnson doesn't take up a trowel and spade to shine light on the long-buried treasures of the ancient world. Instead, she concentrates on reconstructing an anthropological portrait of the most mysterious character of all: the Archaeologist. What drives these archaeologists is not the money (meager) or the jobs (scarce) or the working conditions (dangerous), but their passion for the stories that would otherwise be buried and lost. Her book also highlights the friendships and teamwork she experienced in all the archeological projects she worked on while writing the book.

Marilyn Johnson is also the author of two other works of entertaining non-fiction, *The Dead Beat: Lost Souls, Lucky Stiffs, and the Perverse Pleasures of Obituaries* (Harper Perennial, 2007) and *This Book Is Overdue! How Librarians and Cybrarians Can Save Us All* (Harper Perennial, 2011). Her latest book, *Lives in Ruins,* has been praised by *The New York Times, The Washington Post, The Dallas Morning News, The Austin American-Statesman,* and *Nature,* and was named one of *Publishers Weekly*'s Best Books of 2014. *The Dead Beat* was chosen as a Border's Original Voice and was a finalist for the Barnes & Noble Discover Award, and both *The Dead Beat* and *This Book Is Overdue!* received Washington Irving Book Awards. Johnson is also the author of a recently published article in Smithsonian Magazine highlighting the excavations of the graves of four leaders of the Jamestown Colony. http://www.smithsonianmag.com/smithsonian-institution/new-archaeological-research-jamestown-reveals-identities-four-prominent-settlers-discovery-180956028/?no-ist

Although Johnson lives with her husband, Rob Fleder, near New York City, she will reveal in her talk that she also has strong ties to TEXAS and HOUSTON!

This program was made possible in part with a grant from Humanities Texas, the state affiliate of the National Endowment for the Humanities.

Concurrent Sessions - Saturday Morning

Paluxy

General Session: Archaeology of the Houston Area

8:00 AM   **Search for the Twin Sisters Cannons** - Jorge Garcia-Herreros and Jasmin Talbert

8:20 AM   **Cultural Resource Subsurface Survey and Archeological Monitoring of the Nau Center for Texas Cultural Heritage, Houston, Harris County, Texas** – Eleanor Stoddart

8:40 AM   **Don't Forget the Garbage! Documenting Urban Trash Dumps as Evidence of Municipal Waste Management Practices and Socioeconomic Discrimination** – Doug K. Boyd

9:00 AM   **Canister and Grape: Artillery Related Artifacts from the San Jacinto Battleground** – Douglas G. Mangum

9:20 AM   BREAK

General Session: Archaeology of the Historic Period in Texas

9:40 AM   **A New Beginning for the Old Socorro Mission del Sur** – Tiffany Osburn

10:00 AM   **The San Felipe de Austin Heritage Learning Project: Educational Partnerships and Public Archeology at the Birthplace of Texas** – Jon C. Lohse, Carol Salva, and Brett Cruse

10:20 AM   **A Comparative Analysis of Decorative Ceramics and Choice at the Gregory Lincoln/HSPVA Site and the Levi Jordan Plantation Site** - Lauren Falcon Maas

10:40 AM   **Sawing Logs Once More: The Removal and Restoration of a late 1880s Sawmill on the Zapalac Ranch (41FY430)** – Stephanie Mueller

11:00 AM   **Vandalism and Property Destruction in the 21st Century: Understanding the Challenges of Researching an Historic Cemetery in North Central Texas** – Chris Barry and Catrina Whitley

11:20 AM   **Archaeological Investigations on the West side of Plaza de Armas, San Antonio, Bexar County, Texas** - Clinton M. M. McKenzie

11:40 AM   **Identifying the Archaeological Potential of the Rio Grande Valley Civil War Trail** – Russell K. Skowronek

Concurrent Sessions - Saturday Morning

Permian

Symposium: 2015 Archaeological Investigations at Barnhill Rockshelter #3

8:00 AM   **An Overview of the 2015 Baylor University Archaeological Field School at Barnhill Rockshelter #3 (41CV1646), Coryell County, Texas** – Vincent Villarreal

8:20 AM   **Geoarchaeology and Rockshelter Evolution along McCutchen Branch** – Shane J. Prochnow and Carol Macaulay-Jameson

8:40 AM   **Using Ethnographies to Interpret the Spatial Patterning at Barnhill Rockshelter #3** – William Crisp

9:00 AM   **Use and Delineation of Space within Barnhill Rockshelter #3** – Cassady Holt

9:20 AM   BREAK

9:40 AM   **Use-Wear Analysis of Utilized Flakes from Barnhill Rockshelter #3 (41CV1646)** – Kendall Turner

10:00 AM   **Curing Common Ailments: Medicinal Use of Plants at Barnhill Rockshelter #3** – Sarah Welle

10:20 AM   **Macrobotanical Analysis of the Carbonized Plant Remains Recovered from Three Earth Ovens and a Midden at Barnhill Rockshelter #3 (41VC1646), Coryell County, Texas** – Nicole Beckwith

10:40 AM   **Processing Acorns: "There is nothing to it"** – Gracie Beard and Krissa Green

11:00 AM   BREAK

General Session: The 2015 TAS Field School at the Tait-Huffmeyer Ranch in Columbus, Texas

11:20 AM   **Oh the Weather Outside was Frightful, but the ~~Margarita~~ Company was so Delightful: A Report on the 2015 TAS Field School** – Jason W. Barrett

11:40 AM   **Cotton Field in Context: Some Preliminary Observations on the Site and Its Setting** – Charles D. Frederick

Concurrent Sessions - Saturday Morning

Woodbine

General Session: Perspectives on the Paleoindian and Archaic Periods in Texas

8:00 AM   **Preliminary Results of an Archaeological Survey in Eastern Brewster County** - Caitlin Gulihur

8:20 AM   **Recent Excavations at Knibbe Ranch (41CM363): Looking for a Bison Cliff Jump in Central Texas** - Robert Lassen

8:40 AM   **The Archaic Period of Trans-Pecos Texas and Southern New Mexico: New Insights and New Revelations** - Myles R. Miller and Tim Graves

9:00 AM   **The Timber Fawn Clovis Site, Kingwood, Harris County, Texas** - Wilson W. "Dub" Crook, III

9:20 AM   **The Early Archaic and Paleoindian Occupation of Kelley Cave (41VV164)** - Daniel Rodriguez

9:40 AM   **Clovis Flakes at the Gault Site... It's All in the Platform Baby!** - Nancy V. Littlefield

10:00 AM   **The Who, What, Where, When, and Why of Clovis Blade Manufacturing in Texas** - Thomas Williams

10:20 AM   BREAK

General Session: New Methods in Rock Art Research

10:40 AM   **How to Capture a Photograph Worth a Thousand Words: Photographic Documentation of Rock Art in the Lower Pecos Canyonlands of Texas** – Jerod L. Roberts, Victoria L. Muñoz, and Carolyn E. Boyd

11:00 AM   **Perspectives on Pictographs: Differences in Rock Art Recording Frameworks of the Rattlesnake Canyon Mural** – Audrey K. Lindsay

11:20 AM   **It's not an Illustration; it's a Graphic Database: Rock Art Documentation in the Digital Age** - Lindsay A. Vermillion and Carolyn E. Boyd

11:40 AM   **X-ray Fluorescence Analysis of Rock Art in Big Bend Ranch State Park, Presidio and Brewster Counties, Texas** - Christopher Dostal

TAS Poster Session - Saturday Morning

Texas Ballroom Foyer
8:30 AM – 10:30 AM

TAS Poster Session (Posters will be attended from 8:30 AM – 9:30 AM)

- **Urban Geoarcheology and Site Formation Processes at HemisFair Plaza in San Antonio, Texas** - Steven W. Ahr
- **Rock Imagery on the Pinto Canyon Ranch** - Samuel S. Cason
- **Finding the 370th: The Archaeology of a World War I Training Camp in Houston, Texas** - Dylan Dickens, Rachel George, Jake Krauss, and Jeffrey Fleisher
- **Life along the Brazos: Testing at a Possible Tenant Home near Richmond, Texas** - Anastasia Gilmer and John R. Ferguson
- **A Search for the Henderson Yoakum House Using Historical Documents and Geophysical Survey** - Bryan S. Haley and Douglas G. Mangum
- **Radiocarbon Based Occupation Patterns of the San Antonio River** – Leonard Kemp, Raymond Mauldin, Jason B. Perez, and William Unsinn
- **A Comparison of Two Predictive Models in Abilene State Park, Taylor County, Texas** - Ken Lawrence, Christian Hartnett, Steve Carpenter, Tony Lyle, and Chris Lintz
- **Life of a Central Texas Woman 1000 Years Ago: Clues from the Archaeological Investigations at Barnhill Rockshelter #3 (41CV1646) and from Ethnohistorical Accounts** - Katie Mackenzie
- **Can Flake Size Provide Meaningful Information about Flint Knapping Events?** - Scott Pletka
- **The Index of Texas Archaeology: Open Access Gray Literature from the Lone Star State** - Robert Z. Selden Jr. and Britt Bousman
- **Unique findings within an analysis of a single coprolite from Conejo Shelter, Texas** - Elanor Sonderman, Crystal Dozier, and Morgan Smith
- **Utilizing Archival Information to Re-Locate or "Stumble Upon" Lost Archeological Sites** - Waldo Troell
- **Andean Burial Rites: An Anthropological Study of Human Immolation within Pre-Columbian Inca Society** - Ashley Vance and Molly Minus
- **Long-Term Phosphate Experiment** - Lindsay Vermillion, Ken Lawrence, and Texas State Experimental Archaeology Club
- **Unidentified Ceramics in Southwestern Collections** - Robin Gay Wakeland

Concurrent Sessions - Saturday Afternoon

Paluxy

Symposium: TARL Today: Projects and Prospects

1:30 PM **The Legacy of A.T. Jackson** - Jonathan H. Jarvis

1:50 PM **WPA Archaeology: Revisiting the Harrell Site Collections** - Marybeth S. F. Tomka and Lauren H. Bussiere

2:10 PM **Skeletal Pathologies of Prehistoric Individuals at Falcon Reservoir** - Stacy M. Drake

2:30 PM **The Harrell Site: a new perspective of Prehistoric Cemetery** - Jessie LeViseur

2:50 PM **TARL Today** - Brian E. Roberts

3:10 PM BREAK

Symposium: Big Bend Archaeology

3:30 PM **The Genevieve Lykes Duncan Site: A Late Paleoindian Campsite in the Chihuahuan Desert** - William A. (Andy) Cloud and Richard W. Walter

3:50 PM **The Late Quaternary Stratigraphic Setting of Genevieve Lykes-Duncan Site, O2 Ranch, Brewster County, Texas** - Charles D. Frederick, Brittney Gregory, and David Yelacic

4:10 PM **Archaeology at the Fulcher Site (41BS1495): A Multi-component Open Campsite Along the Lower Reaches of Terlingua Creek, Brewster County, Texas** – Richard W. Walter

4:30 PM **Archaeological Research on the Pinto Canyon Ranch, Presidio County, Texas** - Samuel S. Cason

4:50 PM **The Rock Art and the History of San Esteban Rockshelter, Presidio County, Texas** - Roger Boren

Concurrent Sessions - Saturday Afternoon

Permian

General Session: New Methods and Research in Texas Archaeology

2:00 PM   **Build It and They Will Come: Examining Burned Rock Feature Construction and Re-use During the Late Archaic at 41CV286** - Eric R. Oksanen

2:20 PM   **A GIS Analysis of Alibates Quarries and Antelope Creek Sites - an update** – Britt Bousman, Virginia Moore, and Bob Wishoff

2:40 PM   **A Consideration of Labor Expenditure in Archaic Biface Production in the Rio Grande Plains** - Christopher W. Ringstaff

3:00 PM   **Preliminary Ecologically Diagnostic Xylem Analysis (EDXA) of Mesquite Wood along an East-West Transect Across Texas, and Implications for Ancient Rainfall Patterns** - Kevin Hanselka

3:20 PM   **Archaeological and Geological Test Excavations at Site 41HM61, Hamilton County, Central Texas: Life along the Leon River During Archaic and Late Prehistoric Times** - Richard A. Weinstein, Charles D. Frederick, and Jon C. Lohse

3:40 PM   BREAK

4:00 PM   **Las Camas or Cupboards? An Analysis of Supposed Sleeping Features from Hinds Cave (41VV456) in Val Verde County, Texas** - Casey Wayne Riggs

4:20 PM   **Rethinking Archaeological Field Forms: The Use and Application of Mobile Computing to Collect Archaeological Data** - Christian T. Hartnett

4:40 PM   **Raman Spectroscopy of FCR from Texas Earth Ovens** - Laura Short

5:00 PM   **Holocene Alluvial Stratigraphy and Geoarcheology at Walnut Creek, Central Texas** - Steven W. Ahr

Concurrent Sessions - Saturday Afternoon

Woodbine

Symposium: Trans Rio Bravo/Rio Grande International Research Collaboration

1:30 PM   **50 Years along the Rio Grande: Reflections on a Variety of Archaeological Research Projects on the Border** – Thomas R. Hester

1:55 PM   **Al otro lado del Río Grande: los escasos estudios binacionales en Nuevo León, México. (On the other side of the Rio Grande: the few binational studies of Nuevo Leon, Mexico)** - Moises Valadez Moreno

2:20 PM   **¿Dónde está la frontera? (Where is the Frontier?)** - Victoria L. Muñoz

2:45 PM   **Connections: Rock Art Across the River of Two Names** - William Breen Murray

3:10 PM   **Con un pie en cada lado: Nuevo Santander Ranching Communities** - Mary Jo Galindo

3:35 PM   **Fuentes archivísticas para la etnohistoria del noreste de Mexico y de Texas (Archival Resources for Ethnohistorical Studies of Northeastern Mexico and Texas)** - Martín Salinas Rivera

4:00 PM   **Panel Discussion**

TAS Poster Session - Saturday Afternoon

Texas Ballroom Foyer
11:00 AM – 3:00 PM

Poster Session: Eagle Nest Canyon 2015: Ongoing Investigations
(Posters will be attended from 11:00 AM – 12:00 AM)

- **Botanical preservation in Texas Rockshelters: Eagle Nest Canyon (northeastern Chihuahuan Desert) and McCutchen Branch (Lampasas Cut Plain)** – Leslie L. Bush, Kevin Hanselka, Christina M. Neilsen, Daniel Rodriguez, and Carol A. Macaulay-Jameson

- **Paleofeces at Eagle Cave: Preliminary Report of Ongoing Research** - Stephen L. Black, Emily R. McCuistion, Matthew E. Larson, and Chase W. Beck

- **Texas State University 2015 Field School Investigations at Horse Trail Shelter** - Amanda Castañeda and Charles Koenig

- **Eagle Cave South Trench 2015: Cleaning the Kitchen at Feature 8** - Bryan Heisinger

- **Extending Arenosa Shelter's Reach: Zooarchaeological Research in Eagle Nest Canyon 2015** - Christopher Jurgens and Haley Rush

- **Eagle Cave South Trench 2015: Initial Results from Profile Section 9** - Matthew E. Larsen

- **Eagle Cave South Trench 2015: Profile Section 12** - Emily R. McCuistion

- **2015 Investigations of Eagle Cave** - Charles W. Koenig and Steve L. Black

- **Micromorph Mania: A Microstratigraphic Approach to Evaluating Site Formation Processes at Eagle Cave** - Christina Nielsen, Charles D. Frederick, and Ken Lawrence

- **Eagle Cave South Trench 2015: Initial Observations from PS015** - Victoria C. Pagano

- **Two Independent Methods for Dating Rock Art: Age Determination of Paint and Oxalate Layers at Eagle Cave, TX** – Karen L. Steelman and Carolyn E. Boyd

Saturday Night Banquet Speaker

Jean Clottes
Room: Texas Ballroom
7:00 PM

We are delighted to welcome Dr. Jean Clottes back to Texas as our Banquet speaker for the 86th Annual TAS meeting.

As most of you know, Dr. Clottes is a world renowned expert on prehistoric rock art and has joined us before to discuss rock art in France. This year he is with us to present a program on his latest research on Rock Art and Tribal Art in India. According to Clottes, thousands of painted sites can be found in India and particularly in the center of the country. The spectacular images he will discuss were painted or engraved over a long period of time, dating back to 10,000 years ago.

Dr. Clottes and his associate, Dr. Meenakshi Dubey Pathak have recorded many rock art sites deep in the jungles of central India, where cultural and natural contexts have been well preserved due to their remote settings. They observed ceremonies that are still taking place in the painted shelters and were able to study local tribes and collect detailed testimonies on rapidly vanishing practices and age-old traditions that explain the deeper meanings of the rock art images.

"In the earliest paintings from the Mesolithic period, hunting was most often represented, as well as dancing and animals like peacocks. In the Neolithic/Chalcolithic, cattle took over in the imagery as they were people's riches and were so to speak part of the family. In troubled Historical times, the themes mentioned were still represented but warriors, weapons and fighting became prevalent in the art," said Clottes. "The most obvious purpose for the paintings is about the beneficial power of the images. They are indeed images for the spirits and for the gods, but also for the tribal people themselves who ask for protection from the gods through their paintings and the ceremonial practices that surround them."

Dr. Clottes studied at Toulouse University (1950-1957) and received his PhD in Prehistory in 1975. He was appointed Director of Prehistoric Antiquities for Midi-Pyrenees in 1971. In 1992 he was appointed General Inspector for Archaeology at the Ministry of Culture in France and in 1993 became the Scientific Advisor for everything relating to prehistoric rock art, a position he held until his official retirement in July 1999. He is currently the editor of the International Newsletter on Rock Ara (INORA). He is also an international expert for rock art with ICOMOS (The International Council on Monuments and Sites) and UNESCO (United Nations Educational, Scientific and Cultural Organization).

He has published or edited 31 books and more than 500 papers on the subject of rock art. Five of his books (and many papers) have been published in English including The Cave Beneath the Sea (Harry Abrams, 1996); The Shamans of Prehistory, with D. Lewis-Williams (Harry Abrams 1998); World Rock Art (Getty Foundation, 2002); Chauvet Cave: The Art of Earliest times (ed) (The University of Utah Press, 2003); and Cave Art (Phaidon, 2008, 2010).

Dr. Clottes will also be appearing at the Second Annual TAS Book Festival sponsored by JTAH from 5:00 – 5:50 on Saturday, October 24th, immediately preceding the Banquet. He will discuss his most recent book, published in French with his associate, Dr. Dubey-Pathak and entitled *Des Images pour les Dieux. Art rupestre et Art tribal dans le Centre de l'Inde* (Images for the Gods. Rock art and tribal art in the center of India).

2015 T. A. S. Book Festival

Texas Ballroom Foyer

Friday, October 23

1:00 PM **Douglas Mangum and Roger Moore**
The Archaeology of Engagement: Conflict and Revolution in the United States

2:00 PM **Wilson W. "Dub" Crook, III**
The Late Prehistoric of the East Fork: A Redefinition of Cultural Concepts Along the East Fork of the Trinity River, North Central Texas

3:00 PM **Nancy Kenmotsu and Doug Boyd**
The Toyah Phase of Central Texas: Late Prehistoric Economic and Social Processes

4:00 PM **Marilyn Johnson**
Lives in Ruins: Archaeologists and the Seductive Lure of Human Rubble

Saturday, October 24

9:00 AM **Andrew Hall**
Civil War Blockade: Running on the Texas Gulf Coast

10:00 AM **Mike Waters**
The Hogeye Clovis Cache

11:00 AM **Harry Shafer**
Painters in Prehistory: Archaeology and Art of the Lower Pecos Canyonlands

12:00 PM **BREAK** from 12:00 PM to 2:00 PM
T. A. S. Business Luncheon

2:00 PM **Diana M. Greenlee**
Poverty Point: Revealing the Forgotten City

3:00 PM **Wes Tunnell and Jace Tunnell**
Pioneering Archaeology in the Texas Coastal Bend

4:00 PM **Myriam Arcangeli**
Sherds of History: Domestic Life in Colonial Guadeloupe

5:00 PM **Jean Clottes**
Des images pour les dieux : Art rupestre et art tribal dans le centre de l'Inde
(Images for the Gods. Rock art and tribal art in the center of India)

2015 T. A. S. Book Festival

Organized and sponsored by the
Journal of Texas Archeology and History.org

Greetings!

The *Journal of Texas Archeology and History.org* is pleased to organize and sponsor the 2015 T.A.S. Book Festival as part of the TAS Annual Meeting in Houston. We have a terrific line-up of authors presenting recent new publications of interest to our membership and the general public. The event will begin Friday afternoon, October 23 beginning at 1:00 PM when four authors will present their new books. Friday is topped off by our evening public speaker, Marilyn Johnson, presenting her new book "*Lives in Ruins: Archaeologists and the Seductive Lure of Human Rubble*" at 4:00 PM. On Saturday we will begin at 9:00 AM and will take a break during the TAS business meeting luncheon. After lunch Diana Greenlee will present her new book *"Poverty Point: Revealing the Forgotten City"* about the new World Heritage site, Poverty Point. The book festival will be wrapped up by our banquet speaker, Jean Clottes, presenting his new book on the rock art of India, "Rock Art and Tribal Art in India" ("*Des Images pour les Dieux. Art rupestre et Art tribal dans le Centre de l'Inde*") starting at 5:00 PM. Authors will address the room to discuss their book and the writing process. Afterward, they will be selling and autographing their books. The book festival is open to the public and will take place in the hotel atrium near the book room and silent auction. Following is the schedule and information for the authors presenting their recently published works, links to their websites and publication information:

FRIDAY, October 23, 2015

1:00 PM – 1:50 PM DOUGLAS MANGUM and ROGER MOORE

"The Archaeology of Engagement: Conflict and Revolution in the United States"
Edited by Dana L. Pertermann and Holly K. Norton
Presented by Contributing Authors: Roger G. Moore and Douglas Mangum

When a historic battlefield site is discovered and studied, the focus is often on the "hardware": remnants of weaponry, ammunition, supplies, and equipment that archaeologists carefully unearth, analyze, conserve, and frequently place on display in museums. But what about the "software"? What can archaeology teach us about the humans involved in the conflict: their social mores and cultural assumptions; their use and understanding of power?

In *The Archaeology of Engagement: Conflict and Revolution in the United States*, Dana L. Pertermann and Holly Kathryn Norton have assembled a collection of studies that includes sites of conflicts between groups of widely divergent cultures, such as Robert E. Lee's mid-1850s campaign along the Concho River and the battles of the River Raisin during the War of 1812. Notably, the second half of the book applies the editors' principles of conflict-event theory to the San Jacinto Battlefield in Texas, forming a case study of one of America's most storied—and heavily trafficked—battle sites.

Conflicts, battles in particular, are events that were purposeful, meant to change the present in which the participants lived. Culturally contingent, and often having unforeseen consequences, conflict-event theory recognizes that battles provide rapid social change akin to punctuated equilibrium, complementing a more gradual, daily process of cultural change. As many of the contributions illustrate, archaeology provides new insights to the understanding of battles that traditional historiography is often unable to access. While this book focuses on American battlefields, it will also contribute to the ever-expanding research of cross-cultural violence and warfare.

DANA L. PERTERMANN is associate professor of anthropology and geology at Western Wyoming Community College in Rock Springs. **HOLLY K. NORTON** is a compliance manager for the Colorado Office of Archaeology and Historic Preservation in Denver.

Dr. Roger G. Moore has worked as a professional archeologist since 1976. He was a pioneer in demonstrating the potential for survival of significant archeological remains in heavily urbanized American contexts such as the City of Galveston and the Houston Central Business District, as well as in developing the archeological field methods appropriate for dealing with urban contexts. His work and publication in urban archeology began during his graduate studies at Rice University and has continued throughout his subsequent career. Moore initiated an independent archeological consulting practice based in Houston, Texas, in 1982. His firm has conducted over 500 major archeological projects and many smaller investigations. These projects were conducted for a very diverse array of endeavors including original historical and archeological research, highway construction, mass transit, park development, energy projects, oil spills, flood control, real estate development, industrial development and conflict archeological research at the San Jacinto Battleground.

Moore is also keenly interested in spatial relationships and developed a quantitatively based predictive model for prehistoric settlement in Southeast Texas that has been acknowledged as accurate by the Archeology Division of the Texas Historical Commission. While now eclipsed by the Texas Sites Atlas, his firm had its own internal GIS project of prehistoric site locations, survey areas, historical markers, and other relevant geographical loci in this region years before the introduction of the Atlas. Moore's presentations and peer-reviewed publications in recent years have centered upon his firm's conflict archeological discoveries at San Jacinto.

Douglas Mangum M.A. is a Principal Investigator and Historian at Moore Archeological Consulting. In those capacities he co-manages the work the firm has conducted at the San Jacinto Battlefield. Before joining the firm he worked for the U. S. Forest Service and in various volunteer and student projects that took him to sites in Scotland, England, Mississippi, and New Mexico as well as Texas. Douglas earned his BA in Archeology at the University of Texas and an MA in History from the University of Houston–Clear Lake. Douglas' master's thesis focused on American expansionism in the early nineteenth century, particularly as it applies to Texas. This historical focus and his research into the Battle of San Jacinto, in combination with his archeological work at the battlefield, has resulted in his chapter in the book *The Archaeology of Engagement, Conflict and Revolution in the United States.*

Publisher: Texas A&M University Press, 10/16/2015, ISBN: 978-1-62349-294-6
Links to online sales: http://tamupress.com/product/Archaeology-of-Engagement,8353.aspx
Links to Editor: https://www.westernwyoming.edu/academics/geology/faculty.html (for Pertermann)
Link to Moore Archeological Consultants: http://moore-archeological.com/new/main.htm/

2:00 PM – 2:50 PM WILSON "DUB" CROOK

"The Late Prehistoric of the East Fork: A Redefinition of Cultural Concepts along the East Fork of the Trinity River, North Central Texas"
Wilson W. "Dub" Crook, III and Mark D. Hughston

Over the last 42 years, the authors have studied in detail the sites and archeological remains ascribed to the Late Prehistoric period of the East Fork of the Trinity River and its tributaries. This includes 20 major sites and a larger number of smaller campsites that occur within a 75 km by 15 km north-south corridor from Collin County in the north to northwestern Kaufman County in the south. As part of this study, we have accessed and examined all known collections from previous investigations with a combined artifact assemblage of nearly 32,000 specimens. In addition, we obtained access to the unpublished field notes and maps from many previous researchers and combined them with our own field and laboratory observations. The results of this study confirm the conclusion of previous researchers that the "Wylie Focus", as originally proposed), is an outdated concept. A new chronological sequence consisting of a Woodland period followed by two Late Prehistoric period phases is proposed. In detailing the proposed new sequences, extensive information on each major site, site features such as the distinctive rim-and-pit structures, burials, hearths and caches, and the diagnostic artifacts that characterize each cultural phase are provided. We also detail how the Late Prehistoric of the East Fork is a unique culture, similar but yet distinctly different from all its surrounding neighbors.

Wilson W. "Dub" Crook, III recently retired after a 35 year distinguished career as a Senior Executive with the Exxon Mobil Corporation. Dub has traveled extensively throughout the world, starting his archeological adventures as a child with his father, Wilson W. "Bill" Crook, Jr. who was past President and Fellow of the TAS. A native of Dallas, Dub attended Southern Methodist University where he majored in Geology (Mineralogy). He is the author of over 150 papers in such varied fields as geology, mineralogy, archeology, natural science and the Soviet manned space program. Dub is a Life Member of the Dallas Archeological Society, a Fellow of the Houston Archeological Society, a long-time member of the TAS, the Center for the Study of First Americans, a Life Member of the Gault School of Archaeological Research, a Research Fellow at the Texas Archeological Research Laboratory in Austin, and a Fellow of the Leakey Foundation.

Mark D. Hughston is currently a senior partner and part owner of Brazos Gas, a successful independent oil and gas exploration company in Dallas. A native of North Dallas, Mark attended Southern Methodist University where he majored in Geology and Anthropology. After turning to Petroleum geology in graduate school, Mark has continued his dream of establishing both a successful private business as well as maintaining his research interests in archeology and vertebrate paleontology. He is the author of a number of scientific papers, many with his colleague Dub Crook. Mark is a member of the Dallas, Houston, and Texas Archeological Societies.

Publisher: CreateSpace, a DBA on On-Demand Publishing, LLC (an Amazon Company), Charleston, South Carolina, May 30, 2015, ISBN: 978 1508686521
Sales Link: Amazon.com under "Wilson W. Crook, III"

3:00 PM – 3:50 PM NANCY KENMOTSU and DOUG BOYD

"The Toyah Phase of Central Texas: Late Prehistoric Economic and Social Processes"
Editors: Nancy A. Kenmotsu and Douglas K. Boyd
Contributing authors: John W. Arnn, III, Douglas K. Boyd, Zackary I. Gilmore, Leonard Kemp, Nancy A. Kenmotsu, Karl W. Kibler, Raymond Mauldin, Khori Newlander, Elton R. Prewitt, John D. Speth, and Jennifer Thompson.

This book is an edited volume with 9 chapters presenting a variety of perspectives on the archeology and ethnohistory of the Toyah phase. Texas is particularly suited to the study of hunter-gatherers, for the majority of its lands were home to such groups for thousands of years. *The Toyah Phase of Central Texas* focuses on the hunter-gatherers who occupied at least 25 percent of the state, particularly its central core, just before and during the early incursion of Spain north of the banks of the Rio Grande, a time frame known as the Toyah phase (AD 1300 – 1750). Toyah phase sites have been of great interest to professional and avocational archeologists since they were first recorded and investigated over seventy years ago. Several TAS field schools have investigated Toyah sites, including at Rowe Valley, Mission Espiritu Santo, and, more recently, Area 4 of the Eagle Bluff site. The authors take advantage of previous and recent work on Toyah phase sites, especially a number of recent cultural resource management-sponsored excavations.

Once thought to be a single "cultural group" that spread across a large portion of Texas, it now seems likely that the Toyah phase represents a large social field composed of many different communities that shared a common material culture and lifestyle. The authors examine topics such as what defines the Classic Toyah area and the

variability seen in the peripheral Toyah areas, the archeological evidence for interregional exchange systems, subsistence, the role of intergroup conflicts, and the nature of Toyah society during the dynamic period of early European contact. While this book may not provide definitive answers to all, it does make one step back and think about Toyah's archeological and ethnographic evidence in new ways.

Dr. Nancy A. Kenmotsu is a Senior Archeologist at Versar, Inc. Nancy's primary research interest is how small-scale societies adapt to environmental and cultural change and has studied this topic by examining the impact of Spanish colonization on native populations of hunter-gatherers north and south of the Rio Grande as well as the interaction of the people of La Junta de los Rios (modern Presidio, Texas) with their hunter-gatherer and Puebloan neighbors. She has also studied the history of Native Americans in the Lone Star state from Spanish contact to the early 20th century.

Douglas (Doug) K. Boyd is a Vice President at Prewitt & Associates, Inc., a firm specializing in cultural resource management. Doug has been involved with Texas archeology throughout his life, and he is very interested in the period when native peoples came under influence from European contact and the many changes that they experienced. Born and reared in the Texas Panhandle, Doug has conducted extensive research on the history and prehistory of that region of the state.

Publisher: Texas A&M University Press, College Station, Texas, 2012,
    ISBN: 978-1-60344-690-7 (hard cover), 978-1-60344-755-3 (ebook)
Sales Link: http://www.tamupress.com/product/Toyah-Phase-of-Central-Texas,7113.aspx

4:00 PM – 4:50 PM MARILYN JOHNSON

" Lives in Ruins: Archaeologists and the Seductive Lure of Human Rubble"

Lives in Ruins has been praised for demystifying the profession and reporting on it with clarity and humor. *The Dallas Morning News* wrote: "As archaeologists collect potsherds and spearpoints, Marilyn Johnson became a collector of archaeologists, tracking them to Machu Picchu and to Fishkill, N.Y., to a Caribbean slave plantation and a Philadelphia beer tasting. In *Lives in Ruins*, she sifts and sorts them, unearthing a treasury of rare characters." Sarah Parcak, K. Kris Hirst, *World Archaeology*, *Discover,* and *American Archaeologist* have recommended it, and *Nature* called it a "gem of hands-on reportage."

Marilyn Johnson is not an archaeologist. Besides *Lives in Ruins*, she has written two other books for HarperCollins about people in cultural memory professions: *The Dead Beat*, about obituary writers, and *This Book Is Overdue!* about librarians and archivists. She wrote *Smithsonian* magazine's story about the chancel burials in Jamestown this summer. She lives near New York City. After this conference, she will speak at the Houston Museum of Natural Science October 26th at 2:30 pm.

Publisher: Harper, 2014, ISBN: 978-0062127181
Links to online book sales:
 http://www.indiebound.org/book/9780062127181
Links to author website:
 http://www.marilynjohnson.net/
Social media page:
 https://www.facebook.com/authormarilynjohnson

SATURDAY, October 24, 2015

9:00 AM – 9:50 AM ANDY HALL

"Civil War Blockade Running on the Texas Coast"
Andrew W. Hall

In the last months of the American Civil War, the upper Texas coast became a hive of blockade running. Though Texas was often considered an isolated backwater in the conflict, the Union's pervasive and systematic seizure of Southern ports left Galveston as one of the only strongholds of foreign imports in the anemic supply chain to embattled Confederate forces. Long, fast steamships ran in and out of the city's port almost every week, bound to and from Cuba. Hall ends this tale with an epilogue that describes the efforts of nautical archaeologists to unravel this tale of daring, desperation and profit.

Andy Hall has volunteered with the office of the State Marine Archaeologist at the Texas Historical Commission to help document historic shipwrecks in Texas waters since 1990. He has worked on numerous marine archaeology projects in Texas, notably from 1995 to 2004 on the Denbigh Project, the most extensive excavation and

research program on a Civil War blockade runner in the Gulf of Mexico. In 2001 Hall was part of the inaugural group of volunteer marine archaeological stewards appointed by the Texas Historical Commission, the first group of its kind in the nation. Hall writes and speaks frequently on the subjects of Texas' maritime history and its military conflicts in the 19th century. In 2012 Hall published his first book, The Galveston-Houston Packet: Steamboats on Buffalo Bayou, with the History Press of Charleston, South Carolina. His second book with the History Press, Civil War Blockade Running on the Texas Coast, was released in 2014. Hall was recently appointed an Honorary Texas Navy Admiral in recognition of his work in bringing Texas' maritime history to a wider audience.

Publisher: The History Press, June 2014, ISBN: 978-1626195004
Links to online sales: http://www.amazon.com/Civil-Blockade-Running-Texas-Coast/dp/1626195005
Links to author website: http://maritimetexas.net/wordpress/

10:00 AM – 10:50 AM MIKE WATERS

"The Hogeye Clovis Cache"
Michael Waters and Thomas Jennings

Roughly thirteen thousand years ago, Clovis hunters cached more than fifty projectile points, preforms, and knives at the toe of a gentle slope near present-day Elgin, Bastrop County, in central Texas. Over the next millennia, deposition buried the cache several meters below the surface. The entombed artifacts lay undisturbed until 2003, when commercial sand mining uncovered this stash of ancient tools. This is the story of the Hogeye cache and its remarkable collection of Clovis artifacts–a time capsule from the past.

Ultimately, fifty-two bifaces were recovered from the site. This book provides a well-illustrated, thoroughly analyzed description and discussion of the Hogeye Clovis cache, the projectile points and other artifacts from later occupations, and the geological context of the site, which has yielded evidence of multiple Paleoindian, Archaic, and Late Prehistoric occupations. The cache of tools and weapons at Hogeye, when combined with other sites, allows us to envision a snapshot of life at the end of the last Ice Age.

Dr. Michael R. Waters is the Director of the Center for the Study of the First Americans and Executive Director of the North Star Archaeological Research Program. He is known for his expertise in First American studies and geoarchaeology. Waters has worked on many archaeological field projects in the United States, Mexico, Russia, Jamaica, and Yemen. His current research projects include the Debra L. Friedkin Site, Texas; Coats-Hines Mastodon site, Tennessee; Page-Ladson site, Florida; and the Hueyatlaco site, Mexico. He has authored or co-authored numerous journal articles and book chapters and is the author of Principles of Geoarchaeology: A North American Perspective. Waters received the 2003 Kirk Bryan Award and the 2004 Rip Rapp Archaeological Geology Award given by the Geological Society of America. He was elected a Fellow of the Geological Society of America in 2004.

Publisher: Texas A&M University Press, 3/02/2015, ISBN: 978-1-62349-214-4 (hard cover), 978-1-62349-232-8 (eBook)
Links to online book sales: http://www.tamupress.com/product/Hogeye-Clovis-Cache,8174.aspx
Links to author website: http://www.centerfirstamericans.com/
Links to author website: http://anthropology.tamu.edu/html/profile--michaelwaters.html
Social Media page: Facebook "Center for the Study of the First Americans"

11:00 PM - 11:50 PM HARRY SHAFER

"Painters in Prehistory: Archaeology and Art of the Lower Pecos Canyonlands."
Harry J. Shafer, PhD.

Painters in Prehistory is an updated edition of the book *Ancient Texans: Rockart and Lifeways along the Lower Pecos*. It presents the results of years of research and dedication to the story of the ancient Lower Pecos canyon dwellers, told by scholars, artists, and photographers who have deepened the understanding of the rock art interpretations and life of these prehistoric people. The work draws from leading scholar in the field and on new scientific analysis of artifacts to yield a vivid view of the lifeways of the Lower Pecos Canyonlands.

Harry J. Shafer, PhD., is the new Curator of Archaeology for the Witte Museum. He received a PhD in anthropology from the University of Texas at Austin and has been active in archaeological research for the past 52 years. He is professor emeritus at Texas A&M University and his main research interests are Texas prehistory, the American Southwest (Mimbres and Jornada

Mogollon), and Lowland Maya lithic technology. His is a Texas Archeological Society Fellow and recipient of the society's Lifetime Achievement Award. Shafer has written two books, Ancient Texans: Rock Art and Lifeways of the Lower Pecos and Mimbres Archaeology at the NAN Ranch Ruin. He is the editor of Painters in Prehistory, Archaeology and Art of the Lower Pecos Canyonlands, and is a co-author (with Thomas Hester and Kenneth Feder) of Field Methods in Archaeology. He has authored or co-authored more than 300 articles in scientific journals book chapters, and monographs.

Trinity University Press, 2013. Published in association with the Witte Museum. ISBN 978-1-59534-086-3 (hardcover).

12:00 PM – 1:30 PM BREAK FOR T.A.S. BUSINESS LUNCHEON

2:00 PM – 2:50 PM DIANA GREENLEE

"Poverty Point: Revealing the Forgotten City"
Jenny Ellerbe and Diana M. Greenlee

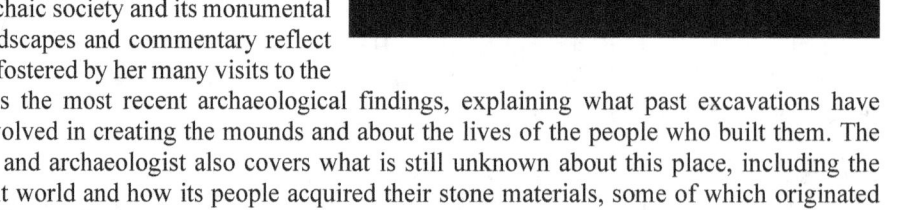

The settlement of Poverty Point, occupied from about 1700 to 1100 BC and once the largest city in North America stretches across 345 acres in northeastern Louisiana. The structural remains of this ancient site—its earthen mounds, semicircular ridges, and vacant plaza—intrigue visitors as a place of inspiration as well as puzzlement. *"Poverty Point: Revealing the Forgotten City"* delves into this enduring piece of Louisiana's cultural heritage through personal introspection and scientific investigation.

With stunning black-and-white photography by Jenny Ellerbe and engrossing text by archaeologist Diana M. Greenlee, this imaginative and informative book explores in full Poverty Point's Late Archaic society and its monumental achievements. Ellerbe's landscapes and commentary reflect the questions and mysteries fostered by her many visits to the site, and Greenlee discusses the most recent archaeological findings, explaining what past excavations have revealed about the work involved in creating the mounds and about the lives of the people who built them. The conversation between artist and archaeologist also covers what is still unknown about this place, including the city's function in the ancient world and how its people acquired their stone materials, some of which originated over a thousand miles from Poverty Point.

The historical significance of Poverty Point, which was recognized by UNESCO as a World Heritage Site in 2014, resonates regionally, nationally, and internationally.

Jenny Ellerbe has spent most of her photographic career exploring and documenting the largely overlooked region surrounding her hometown of Monroe, Louisiana. She is a self-taught photographer whose photographs have been published in journals such as *Lenswork Magazine, The Oxford American, Science, Louisiana Life, and Louisiana Cultural Vistas.* Her work resides in the permanent collections of the Masur Museum of Art, Monroe, Louisiana, and the Museum of Fine Arts, Houston, Texas, as well as private collections in the US and Canada.

Diana M. Greenlee, Ph.D., is the Station Archaeologist at the Poverty Point World Heritage Site and an Adjunct Professor of Archaeology in the School of Sciences at the University of Louisiana at Monroe (ULM). She earned her Ph.D. in Anthropology from the University of Washington in Seattle in 2002 and has been the Poverty Point Station Archaeologist since August 2006. In recognition of her contributions to the effort to place Poverty Point on the World Heritage List, she was named the 2013 Archaeologist of the Year by the Lieutenant Governor of Louisiana.

Publisher: LSU Press, April 2015, ISBN: 978-0807160213
Links to online book sales: http://lsupress.org/books/detail/poverty-point/
Links to author website: http://www.jennyellerbe.com/
Facebook at:
http://www.facebook.com/#!/pages/Poverty-Point-Station-Archaeology-Program/175315712487100
Poverty Point World Heritage Initiative:
http://www.crt.state.la.us/cultural-development/archaeology/discover-archaeology/poverty-point-world-heritage-site/index

3:00 PM – 3:50 PM WES and JACE TUNNELL

"Pioneering Archaeology in the Texas Coastal Bend: The Pape-Tunnell Collection"
John W. Tunnell Jr. and Jace W. Tunnell
With a foreword by Thomas R. Hester and contributions from Harold F. Pape, John W. Tunnell Sr., and Thomas R. Hester

When Harold F. Pape moved to Gregory, Texas, in 1927, he quickly became fascinated by the wealth of Native American artifacts along the nearby shoreline of Corpus Christi Bay and what is now called Port Bay, a southern arm of the larger Copano Bay. A lifelong natural history enthusiast and collector, Pape met and married Lucile H. Tunnell, a widow with three young sons. Before long, John W. Tunnell, Lucile's oldest son, was accompanying Pape on his field studies in surrounding areas and the wider Texas Coastal Bend.

Working in the days before much of the development that now covers the region, Pape and Tunnell studied more than two hundred sites throughout the Coastal Bend, making meticulous logs, maps, and notes of their discoveries.

John W. (Wes) Tunnell Jr. and Jace Tunnell have organized and documented their family collection and present it, along with brief biographies of the two collectors, as a survey of the state of knowledge in the late 1920s and 1930s, as well as a tribute to these two important early researchers and their body of work.

JOHN W. (WES) TUNNELL JR. is associate director and endowed chair of biodiversity and conservation science at the Harte Research Institute for Gulf of Mexico Studies and regents' professor, Fulbright scholar, and Professor Emeritus of biology at Texas A&M University–Corpus Christi.

JACE W. TUNNELL, formerly director of research and planning at the Coastal Bend Bays and Estuaries Program, is the director of the Mission-Aransas National Estuarine Research Reserve, where he oversees research, environmental monitoring, and educational outreach.

Publisher: Texas A&M University Press, 5/5/15, ISBN: 978-1-62349-274-8
Sales Link: http://www.tamupress.com/product/Pioneering-Archaeology-in-the-Texas-Coastal-Bend,8189.aspx

4:00 PM – 4:50 PM MYRIAM ARCANGELI

"Sherds of History: Domestic Life in Colonial Guadeloupe"
Myriam Arcangeli

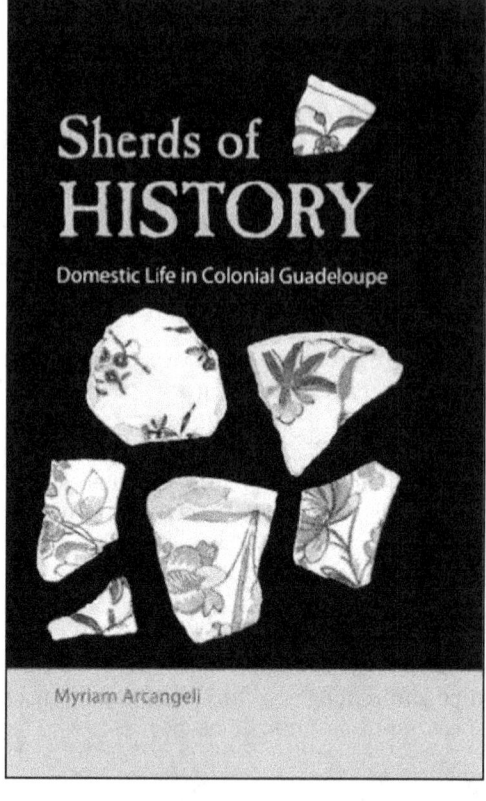

Ceramics serve as one of the best-known artifacts excavated by archaeologists. They are carefully described, classified, and dated, but rarely do scholars consider their many and varied uses. Breaking from this convention, Myriam Arcangeli examines potsherds from four colonial sites in the Antillean island of Guadeloupe to discover what these everyday items tell us about the people who used them. In the process, she reveals a wealth of information about the lives of the elite planters, the middle and lower classes, and enslaved Africans.

By analyzing how the people of Guadeloupe used ceramics--whether jugs for transporting and purifying water, pots for cooking, or pearlware for eating--Arcangeli spotlights the larger social history of Creole life. What emerges is a detail rich picture of water consumption habits, changing foodways, and concepts of health. *Sherds of History* offers a compelling and novel study of the material record and the "ceramic culture" it represents to broaden our understanding of race, class, and gender in French-colonial societies in the Caribbean and the United States.

Arcangeli's innovative interpretation of the material record will challenge the ways archaeologists analyze ceramics.

Myriam Arcangeli recently earned her doctorate in historical archaeology from Boston University. Her research on colonial-era ceramics in Guadeloupe–the basis for this book–explored the history of Creole culture and proposed a novel and original approach for analyzing and interpreting ceramics. Myriam has been interested in ceramics since the beginning of her career, and her first research projects examined the history of local potteries near Toulouse, in southwestern France. Intrigued by the colonial period, she then left for the United States, where she discovered American archaeology while excavating at Mount Vernon, the plantation home of George Washington. Currently, she is working on publishing her research in both French and English journals, and contributed to the forthcoming *The Archaeology of Food: An Encyclopedia*, edited by Mary C. Beaudry and Karen B. Metheny.

Publisher: University Press of Florida, 2/3/2015, ISBN: 978-0-8130-6042-2
Links to online book sales: http://www.upf.com/book.asp?id=ARCAN001
Social media page: https://bu.academia.edu/MyriamArcangeli

5:00 PM – 5:50 PM JEAN CLOTTES

"Rock Art and Tribal Art in India" ("Des Images pour les Dieux. Art rupestre et Art tribal dans le Centre de l'Inde")

Jean Clottes, Foix, France

Thousands of painted sites exist in India, particularly in the center of the country. Those often spectacular images have been painted over a long period, mostly from around 10,000 years ago to Historical times. In the Mesolithic, hunting was most often represented, as well as dancing and animals, such as peacocks. In the Neolithic/Chalcolithic, cattle took over in the imagery. In the troubled Historical times, the themes mentioned above were still represented, but warriors, weapons and fighting became prevalent in the art.

One of the main interests of Indian rock art, that is often not well known because it is in far away, deep jungles, is that its cultural and natural contexts have mostly been preserved. It thus becomes possible to discover among local tribes the persistence of age-old traditions that may have to do with the rock art and explain some of its deeper meanings.

Our research about the tribes that we came into contact with (Korkus, Gonds, Kols, Bhils) focused on two major points. First, the traditional art is still in use today, for example, for funerary ceremonies or to protect people's houses, such as, the murals of the Bhils that have analogies to, and allow for comparison with, rock art. Secondly, we found out that ceremonies with offerings were still going on in some painted shelters, a fact unnoticed until now. We could for the first time collect testimonies on those rapidly vanishing practices and their meanings.

The most obvious purpose of the art concerns the beneficial power of the images. They are indeed images for the gods, but also, and most of all, for the tribal people themselves who ask for their protection through their paintings and the ceremonial practices around them.

Jean Clottes studied at Toulouse University (1950-1957), taught French for three years in England and received his PhD (Doctorat d'Etat) in Prehistory in 1975. He was appointed Director of Prehistoric Antiquities for Midi-Pyrénées in 1971. In 1992, he was appointed General Inspector for Archaeology at the Ministry of Culture, and in 1993 became Scientific Advisor at the same Ministry for everything relating to prehistoric rock art, a position he held until his official retirement in July, 1999.

He is currently the editor of the *International Newsletter on Rock Art* (INORA) He has taught at the Universities of Toulouse (France), Neuchâtel (Switzerland), Gerona (Spain), Buenos Aires (Argentina, INAPL), Berkeley (USA) and Victoria (Canada). He is also an International Expert for rock art with ICOMOS and UNESCO.

His scientific concerns are now mostly related to prehistoric rock art, and in particular, to its preservation and recording, dating problems, the study of its archaeological context (to put it in a better anthropological and cultural perspective), and finally -- and even, mostly -- the problems of epistemology and the search for meaning, particularly in the light of ethnological approaches.

He has published (or edited) 31 books and more than 500 papers. Five of his books (and many papers) have been published in English: *The Cave Beneath the Sea* (Harry Abrams, 1996); *The Shamans of Prehistory*, with D. Lewis-Williams (Harry Abrams, 1998); *World Rock Art* (Getty Foundation, 2002); *Chauvet Cave: the art of earliest times* (ed.) (The University of Utah Press, 2003) ; *Cave Art* (Phaidon, 2008, 2010).

Publisher: Actes Sud, Les éditions Errance, 2013, Arles, France.

Trans Rio Bravo/Rio Grande International Research Collaboration Symposium and Panel Discussion

Organized and sponsored by the *Journal of Texas Archeology and History.org*

Greetings!

The *Journal of Texas Archeology and History.org* is pleased to organize and sponsor the ***"Trans-Rio Bravo/Rio Grande International Research Collaboration Symposium and Panel Discussion"***. The symposium is designed to explore the dearth of archeological research collaboration between two seemingly isolated groups of researchers who are geographically separated only by a thin channel of water that happens to be an international border. There is precious little direct involvement between researchers in Mexico and Texas. This is astounding considering we share a border that is 1,254 miles long!

We hope this event will promote goodwill between the two isolated groups of researchers: Texans and Mexicans. Four guest researchers have been invited to travel from their homes and work in Mexico to participate in this symposium and to engage with us during the TAS Annual Meeting.

Arguably, there is a critical lack of cooperation and collaboration between researchers in Texas and Mexico who are studying archeology and history of the region. Our objectives are threefold: to create a starting point for discussion of the subject; to act as a spring-board toward greater and more meaningful research collaboration in the future; and to open new channels of communication between the two groups.

Through this symposium and panel discussion, we propose to: Facilitate a dialogue regarding issues challenging current and future archeological research collaboration with perspectives presented by participants from both sides of the international border; and to throw a spotlight on recent archeological research along the international boundary region shared by Texas and Mexico where there has either been benefit from successful collaboration or where a project could be enhanced by "trans-Rio Bravo collaboration". Our goals are to: promote an open dialogue between to two isolated groups of researchers; to hold a discussion of the limiting factors in open forum; to explore ways to address or overcome the hurdles faced by modern researchers of archeology in the region; and to promote future collaborative efforts.

The Panel Discussion will follow the final paper and will cover topics relevant to collaboration between researchers across the international boundary line between Texas and Mexico. These topics may include, but are not limited to: language barrier, logistics, safety, publication, funding, access, travel, information sharing, communications, politics, etc.

Discussion will be co-directed by Dr. Todd Ahlman, Director of CAS and Sr. Gustavo Ramirez Castilla, Tamaulipas State Archeologist for INAH. Discussants will include: Tom Hester, Moises Valadez, Victoria L. Munoz, Breen Murray, Mary Jo Galindo and Martin Salinas. Dr. Jean Clottes will be included if he is available for the discussion. A generous grant from the Summerlee Foundation has made this symposium possible.

SATURDAY, October 24, 2015
1:30 PM – 1:50 PM   THOMAS R. HESTER
"50 Years Along the Rio Grande: Reflections on a Variety of Archaeological Research Projects on the Border."

For 50 years, I have taken part in numerous of archaeological studies along the middle and upper Rio Grande. I briefly review a number of these here, with emphasis on those that have involved participation of colleagues in Mexico. These activities began, unfortunately, with digging into Rio Grande rockshelters while in high school! After enrolling at UT-Austin, the focus of fieldwork shifted. In 1967, I was involved in the salvage of Mexican War dead, a saga that continued many years and involved the public and the Mexican government. In the 1970s, I helped conduct extensive excavations at the Spanish missions at Guerrero, Mexico. Later, students and I recorded a rock art site rare on the middle Rio Grande. In the 1970s-1990s, I worked with collectors and avocationals on both sides of the border to document and help them publish important finds. During this period and up to today, I conducted obsidian sourcing studies involving the lower Rio Grande. In 1995, I was part of a large team recording the damage to Falcon Reservoir sites during a serious drought. Also in the 1990's, I worked on a project involving the illegal importation of Mexican artifacts, culminating in a major conference and exhibit in Laredo. Through these projects, I have learned much about the border and interaction with colleagues on both sides of the Rio Grande.

Dr. Thomas R. Hester (Professor of Anthropology, emeritus; The University of Texas at Austin) received his BA from UT-Austin, 1969 and his Ph.D., UC-Berkeley, 1972. For more than 30 years, he taught at UT-San Antonio and UT-Austin, and was director of the UTSA Center for Archaeological Research and the UT-Austin Texas Archeological Research Laboratory. He has done extensive fieldwork and publication in Texas; Belize, Spanish Colonial studies in Mexico and Texas, and has worked in Egypt, California, and Montana. Nearly 700 publications have resulted. He received the SAA's Award for Excellence in Lithic Studies, and Lifetime Achievement Awards from both the Southern Texas Archaeological Association and the Texas Archeological Society.

Email: secocreek@swtexas.net

Social media: Facebook; ResearchGate

1:55 PM – 2:15 PM   MOISES VALADEZ MORENO

"On the Other Side of the Rio Grande: the Few Binational Studies on Nuevo Leon, Mexico."

Unlike other areas such as Chihuahua, Sonora or Baja California, the northeastern region of Mexico has been characterized by the scarcity and little interest from U.S. researchers for the development of archaeological studies. This situation is explained by the lack of communication and binational agreements that facilitate the participation of fellow Texans in the INAH projects, as well as the access of Mexican archaeologists to projects being developed in Texas.

This presentation will review the archaeological survey and excavation projects that have been undertaken during the past 25 years in Nuevo Leon, showing the type of sites and material remains characteristic of this region. The talk will conclude with a discussion of possible agreements and binational projects that could be performed on both sides of the Rio Grande.

Dr. Moises Valadez Moreno is the Profesor Investigador del Instituto Nacional de Antropología e Historia en Nuevo León (INAH Nuevo León).

Email: moisesvaladez@hotmail.com / moisesvaladez@gmail.com

2:20 PM - 2:40 PM   VICTORIA L. MUNOZ

"¿Dónde está la frontera?"

Shumla Archaeological Research and Education Center is working with Mexican historians, archaeologists and iconographers to design a set of procedures and techniques suitable for the documentation, classification, analysis, and interpretation of rock art on both sides of the border. This multi-year collaborative project is funded by Mexico's National Council of Science and Technology, as well as grants received by Shumla. It engages over 20 individuals from both countries, including accomplished researchers and students. Through this partnership, we hope to bridge the gap not only between Mexico and Texas, but also between comparable data sets from our two countries to better understand the hunter-gatherers of this vast region. It's clear that the Rio Grande did not serve as an impenetrable boundary in prehistory and we are limiting ourselves by formulating hypotheses with only a fraction of the data. Shumla will be providing on-site technical training on rock art documentation both in Mexico and in the Lower Pecos. Our Mexican colleagues will be disseminating project results through a permanent seminar, an annual conference, and specialized publications.

Victoria (Vicky) L. Muñoz graduated in 2013 from Texas State University with a B.S. in Anthropology and a minor in Biology. She has worked for Shumla Archaeological Research & Education Center since her graduation, first as an intern and now as a Staff Archaeologist. Vicky serves as Lab Manager, in charge of the day-to-day lab activities. She is also the Database Administrator managing the terabytes of data that Shumla collects and organizing Shumla's ever-growing rock art database. This includes maintenance and IT management of all interfaces used in the lab and field. Vicky's interests in archaeology include the use of digital technologies in the field, GIS, hunter-gatherers, and basketry and weaving technology, to name a few. She is thrilled to live in the "metropolis" of Comstock, Texas and have the opportunity to work with Shumla on the cutting-edge of high-tech rock art research.

Email: Vmunoz@shumla.org

Website: www.shumla.org

Social Media: http://www.facebook.com/SHUMLA

2:45 PM – 3:05 PM   WILLIAM BREEN MURRAY

"Connections: Rock Art Across the River of Two Names"

The river with two names (the Rio Grande/Río Bravo) is a formidable north/south political barrier today but in prehistory it seems to have been a significant east-west connection between the continental interior and the Northeast Mexican corridor of the Sierra Madre Oriental and adjoining Gulf Coastal Plain. This paper will explore connections between Texas rock art sites and that found in the Mexican states of Coahuila and Nuevo León, indicating shared motifs and similarities in site contexts.

Dr. William Breen Murray is Professor Emeritus, Department of Social Sciences, University of Monterrey. Born in Chicago, Illinois (USA). B.A., Carleton College, Northfield, Minnesota (1962); Master's degree (1973) and Ph.d. (1982), Department of Anthropology, McGill University, Montreal, PQ, Canada. Latin American Teaching Fellow, Universidad de Monterrey (1973 1975), Professor of Plant (1976-2006), Department Head of Social Sciences (1978-1992). Rock art Northeastern researcher since 1977 with over 40 articles on the topic published in Mexico, United States, England, Germany, France, Poland, Bulgaria, Chile, Bolivia and China. Compiler of Rock Art of the Northeast (2007), co-editor in Rock Art and Sacred Landscapes (2013); Member of the Board, American Rock Art Research Association (ARARA) (2004-2008); Editor in painting (official organ of ARARA) since 2005.

3:10 PM – 3:30 PM   MARY JO GALINDO

"Con un pie en cada lado: Nuevo Santander Ranching Communities"

Before the Río Grande valley became a contested border between the United States and Mexico, and between predominantly Latino and Anglo- American societies, it was the northern frontier of Spanish Nuevo Santander and a border between Spanish Mexico and indigenous societies to the north. Between 1748 and 1755, the civilian colonists of Nuevo Santander established 23 communities, including 6 along the banks of the Río Grande. The *pobladores*, or colonists, and their descendants had to adapt constantly to the changing political, economic, and social environment, as people in borderlands always do. These *pobladores* received *porciones*, or land grants, on both banks of the river, and they and their descendants literally lived *con un pie en cada lado*, with a foot on each side of the Río Grande. Thus, these ranches were among the first of their kind in present-day Texas, representing a unique form of civilian colonization based on the relocation of entire families, and without major emphasis on missions or presidios. Descendants of these colonists in the Lower Rio Grande Valley still maintain connections to the land and artifacts from their ranches have been used in recent years to teach school-age children about the local history.

Dr. Mary Jo Galindo is a senior principal investigator and project manager in Atkins' Austin office with extensive knowledge of the important historic and archaeological resources of Texas and the border region of southern Texas and northeastern Mexico. She has more than 18 years of experience conducting archaeological surveys, testing, data recovery, and traditional cultural property projects to assure compliance with local, state, and federal laws. She has worked throughout Texas, Oklahoma, Louisiana, Mexico, and Belize. Before joining Atkins, Dr. Galindo served as a regional archaeologist for the Texas Department of Transportation and the Texas Parks and Wildlife Department. She is currently President of the Texas Archeological Society and Chair of the City of Austin Historic Landmark Commission.

Email: Mary.Galindo@Atkinsglobal.com

Website: http://repositories.lib.utexas.edu/bitstream/handle/2152/589/galindomj039.pdf

3:35 PM – 3:55 PM   MARTIN SALINAS RIVERA

"Archival Resources for Ethnohistorical Studies of northeastern Mexico and Texas"

The ethnohistorical knowledge of the Native American populations in the geographic area that now includes the states of Tamaulipas, Nuevo Leon, Coahuila and Texas comes from disseminated archives in the Americas and Europe. Part of their existence lingers from episodes of exploration and colonization of this vast territory that was slowly occupied by the European and novohispanic sociopolitical structure, since the first half of the sixteenth century. Knowledge of the Native Americans in the Coastal Plain and neighboring areas was sporadically recorded. The archival resources are essential to rebuilding their historical presence, adaptations, and cultural changes during colonization, as well as their social decline. This work presents the available archival resources that might be of interest to communities and academics from a variety of disciplines such as cultural anthropology, history, Native American studies, archaeology, ecology, linguistics, and other related disciplines.

Dr. Martin Salinas Rivera is the official historian for the city of Reynosa, Tamaulipas, Mexico, and author of *Indians of the Rio Grande Delta: Their Role in the History of Southern Texas and Northeastern Mexico*, a seminal work based on innumerable primary documents in various Texan and Mexican archives. Dr. Salinas has compiled data on more than six dozen named groups that inhabited the area in the sixteenth through the eighteenth centuries. Depending on available information, he reconstructs something of their history, geographical range and migrations, demography, language, and culture. He also offers general information on various unnamed groups of Indians, on the lifeways of the indigenous peoples, and on the relations between the Indian groups and the colonial Spanish missions in the region.

Email:cronistareynosa@yahoo.com.mx / martinsalinasrivera@yahoo.com.mx

Websites:http://utpress.utexas.edu/index.php/books/salhis#sthash.kTBPsRCA.dpuf

http://www.reynosa.gob.mx/archivo-municipal/index.html

4:00 PM – 5:00 PM   PANEL DISCUSSION

An outstanding panel of researchers working along both sides of the Rio Bravo/Rio Grande will assemble to explore the challenges and prospects of archeological research along our 1,254 mile international border.

CO-MODERATORS: Dr. Todd M. Ahlman
Sr. Gustavo Ramirez Castilla
PANELISTS: Dr. Thomas R. Hester
Dr. Moises Valadez Moreno
Victoria L. Munoz
Dr. William Breen Murray
Dr. Mary Jo Galindo
Dr. Martin Salinas Rivera
SPECIAL PANELIST: Dr. Jean Clottes

5:00 PM – 6:00 PM   PRESIDENT'S RECEPTION

After the panel discussion, the panelists will join the "President's Reception" in the hotel lobby where our guest discussants and co-moderator from Mexico will be honored. They will be available to take your questions and continue the discussion.

PANEL DISCUSSION CO-MODERATORS

Gustavo A. Ramirez Castilla (M.A. Restoration of Monuments (EN-CRyM), Anthropologist with a Major in Archaeology (University of Veracruz), is a researcher with the National Institute of Anthropology and History of Mexico (INAH) at the State of Tamaulipas. In 2009, he founded the Mexican Network of Archaeology or RMA (http://remarq.ning.com/), an organization devoted to the free exchange of information between professional archaeologists and related disciplines with over 4000 worldwide members. For over 27 seven years, Gustavo has worked in salvage archaeology in Mexico on restoration projects in Mitla, Chichen Itza, Las Flores and Tammapul. Mr. Ramirez has conducted research regarding technology, site typology, rock art and mummies of the hunter-gatherer peoples of northeastern Mexico. He has also specialized on the Huastec Culture, conducting many surveys and excavations in that region. Over the last nine years he has directed the excavation of Chak Pet, a Pre-classic Huastecan Coastal Village in Altamira, circa 900 B.C – 200 A.D. In 2003, he led the team who created the Museum of Huastec Culture at Tampico city (http://www.inah.gob.mx/boletines/264-red-de-museos/5830-museo-de-la-cultura-huasteca). Mr. Ramirez has written many popular articles and books about archaeology of Tamaulipas, including Conservation and Cultural Policies (http://gustavoramirezc.blogspot.mx/p/trayectoria.html) and is member of the scientific board of the International Colloquium on Northeastern Mexico and Texas and the International Meeting on Rock Art at Tamaulipas.

Dr. Todd M. Ahlman (Ph.D. University of Tennessee) is the Director of the Center for Archaeological Studies (CAS) at Texas State University. He is an anthropological archaeologist who has over 25 years of experience working on projects across the United States and Caribbean. His experience includes projects in Texas as well as the Northwestern, Plains, Midwestern and Southeastern United States that involve historic and prehistoric archaeological survey, evaluation, and data recovery, and laboratory analyses of prehistoric and historical artifacts. As CAS Director he manages compliance-related and research projects and involves students and recent graduates on these projects to prepare them for successful careers in the public and private sectors. Dr. Ahlman is currently leading a multi-year study archaeological study of the Spring Lake Site in Hays County, Texas that is examining the intact Middle Archaic Calf Creek occupation with future plans to investigate the Paleoindian and Early Archaic occupations.

Symposia Abstracts

Eagle Nest Canyon 2015: Ongoing Investigations (Poster Symposium, 11:00am – 3:00pm Saturday, Texas Ballroom Foyer)

Chairs: Stephen L. Black (Texas State University) and Charles W. Koenig (Texas State University)

Since 2013 Texas State University's Ancient Southwest Texas Project and collaborating research specialists, graduate and undergraduate students, interns, and volunteers have been carrying out new multi-disciplinary investigations in and around Eagle Nest Canyon, a storied locale in the western Lower Pecos Canyonlands at Langtry, Texas. This integrated poster session highlights the ongoing 2015 investigations and preliminary results.

Big Bend Archaeology (Contributed Papers, 4:00pm – 5:40pm Saturday, Paluxy)

Chair: William A. (Andy) Cloud (Center for Big Bend Studies, Sul Ross State University)

Over a decade ago, the Center for Big Bend Studies (CBBS) of Sul Ross State University established the Trans-Pecos Archaeological Program (TAP) to conduct research of the archaeologically rich Big Bend region. Guided by seven thematic research domains, the program is designed to evaluate and integrate past archaeological research in a manner that identifies weaknesses in the regional database, prioritizes research needs, and maximizes present and future scientific data recovery efforts. Through numerous surveys and excavations conducted under the auspices of TAP, the CBBS has made progress in an overarching goal of the program: to bring the region back into the mainstream of archaeological inquiry. The papers in this symposium will highlight some of the exciting research projects conducted through the program.

Trans Rio Bravo/Rio Grande International Research Collaboration (Contributed Papers and Pannel Discussion, 2:00pm – 5:30pm Saturday, Woodbine)

Chair: Steve Davis (Journal of Texas Archeology and History)

The *Journal of Texas Archeology and History.org* is presenting this symposium centered on international collaboration with generous financial support provided by the Summerlee Foundation. Texas shares a 1,254 mile long international border with Mexico, and significant archeological resources, representing over 13,000 years of human occupation, are found on both sides of our shared border along its entire length. Prehistoric populations lived, hunted, and engaged in their daily pursuits using the river as a source of food, water, transportation, and perhaps inspiration. Importantly, the Rio Grande/Rio Bravo did not divide culture groups as it does today, and our predecessors appear to have traveled freely across and along its path. However, comprehensive study of past human occupation in the region has been severely limited due to a number of complicating factors, including international travel restrictions, language differences, safety, site access, politics, funding, and the lack of an information sharing tradition between scholars on either side of the border.

This symposium is populated by participants who are conducting archeological research on both the north and south side of the international border. Papers will highlight successful past research collaborations, as well as projects where the resulting research would have been better served had such collaboration occurred. A roundtable panel will convene immediately following the final paper to discuss topics relevant to collaboration between researchers across the international boundary line between Texas and Mexico.

3D Data in Archaeology (Contributed Papers, 4:00pm – 5:20pm Friday, Woodbine)

Chair: Charles W. Koenig (Texas State University)

Archaeologists across the world have been incorporating more and more 3D data to document and analyze archaeological artifacts, features, sites, and landscapes. This recent trend has penetrated Texas archaeology for research, resource management, and preservation projects. This symposium presents different ways archaeologists working in Texas are not only collecting 3D data, but also using the data for subsequent analyses. Presentations highlight different methodological approaches and future avenues for analysis using 3D data.

2015 Archaeological Investigations at Barnhill Rockshelter #3 (Contributed Papers, 8:00am – 11:00am Saturday, Permian)

Chair: Carol Macaulay-Jameson (Baylor University)

Barnhill Rockshelter #3 (41CV1646), located in Coryell County, has been the focus of Baylor University's archaeological field schools since 2011. The papers in this symposium present the research conducted this summer. Vince Villarreal provides an overview and synthesis of what we have learned from our excavations to date. Shane Prochnow's paper discusses the evolution of the rockshelter and the geoarchaeology of McCutchen Branch. Will Crisp presents a review of the ethnoarchaeological research conducted in rockshelters and how these studies can provide a framework by which to study the use of space within rockshelters. Cassady Holt uses ArcMap to isolate areas where the inhabitants retooled, processed animal carcasses and boiled food. Kendall Turner's research sought to understand how utilized-flake tools were used at the rockshelter, based on microscopic use-wear analysis of experimentally-used tools. Two papers focus on the macrobotanical remains recovered through flotation and identified by Leslie Bush. Sara Welle examines the medicinal uses of the plants recovered and how they might have been used to cure common ailments suffered by the prehistoric inhabitants. Nicole Beckwith presents the results of her comparative study of the botanical remains recovered from three earth ovens at the site. Gracie Beard and Krissa Green's presentation chronicles their experiment from processing acorns to cooking acorn cakes, emulating the process used by Native Californians.

From Burned Rock Features to Battlefields: Current Investigations of the Texas Archeological Stewards Network (Contributed Papers, 2:00pm – 4:00pm Friday, Paluxy)

Chair: Rebecca Shelton (Texas Historical Commission)

The Texas Archeological Stewards Network is thriving in its 31st year and the membership continues to work tirelessly to preserve our shared heritage throughout the state. Many of the Stewards do not conduct their work independently, but collaborate with local communities, private landowners, and regional societies to identify and record sites. The papers presented today offer a glimpse of the extensive impact and outreach the network provides, and show the diversity of work that the network is called to participate in. Ongoing TASN projects include: emergency salvage excavations with the Houston Archeological Society at the Kellum Noble House in Houston; excavations and analysis of the Kemosabe site complex , which is a group of Early Archaic to Toyah phase sites adjacent to the Guadalupe River; documentation of an early Norwegian homestead in Bosque County that was nominated for the National Register of Historic Places; and the identification and cataloguing of artifacts from the lost townsite of San Jacinto near the San Jacinto Battlefield.

TARL Today: Projects and Prospects (Contributed Papers, 2:00pm – 3:40pm Saturday, Paluxy)

Chair: Marybeth S. F. Tomka (Texas Archaeological Research Lab)

This symposium strives to introduce TARL to the TAS audience through a series of papers detailing our staff's latest projects and a presentation from our director on our strategy for the 21st century. TARL staff, students and volunteers are undertaking some new and exciting projects involving old collections and making our holdings available to researchers.

Discussion Group Abstract

TxDOT Roadside Chat with the Caddo Nation of Oklahoma: Discovering Caddo Heritage (3:00pm - 5:00pm Friday, Wilcox)

Organizer: Laura Cruzada (Texas Department of Transportation)

As the Texas Department of Transportation implements projects, it works closely with federally recognized tribes and other parties who have an interest in Texas' history and cultural resources. Because of northeast Texas' rich cultural heritage and history, multiple prehistoric and historic Caddo sites have been discovered over the past 50 years, revealing a remarkable past for this people and Texas. This panel includes the Museum Director of the Caddo Nation of Oklahoma, who will talk about the tribal perspective on archeology as well as exciting outreach projects that the tribe is working on to promote Caddo heritage. TxDOT will discuss outreach activities and recent archeological findings, including one recent project where archeologists re-discovered a lost Caddo site. Lastly, participants will consider the importance of cultural sensitivity when dealing with resources that are sacred to the Native American tribes in order to foster broader understanding and empathy in archeological studies.

Paper and Poster Abstracts

A

Plugging Away: An Update on TxDOT's Geoarcheological Mapping Program (Paper, General Session –Geo-spatial Mapping and Remote Sensing, 2:20pm Friday, Woodbine)

James T. Abbott (Texas Department of Transportation)

TxDOT initiated its district-based geoarcheological mapping program in 1997, and the first model (the Houston-PALM) was published in 2001. Originally produced with hand-mapping, the first models took years to bring to fruition, but in the last few years the production process has been accelerated using new methods. This presentation will discuss the goals and status of the program, and the results of evaluation of the models against the existing site database.

Urban Geoarcheology and Site Formation Processes at HemisFair Plaza in San Antonio, Texas (Poster, Saturday 8:30am-10:30am, Texas Ballroom Foyer)

Steve Ahr (URS/AECOM)

The integrity potential of archeological sites in urbanized settings is often discounted because of the presumption that prior disturbances have compromised the natural stratigraphic and pedologic setting in which archeological materials may be found. In order to evaluate the degree to which development has impacted archeological deposits in the downtown San Antonio area, archival research, construction monitoring, and geoarcheological investigations were conducted as part of the city's Market Street realignment project. This integrated approach resulted in the reconstruction of the natural and cultural site formation history of the project area, and revealed remarkable site preservation conditions immediately below a shallow zone of artificial fill material.

Holocene Alluvial Stratigraphy and Geoarcheology at Walnut Creek, Central Texas (Paper, General Session – New Methods and Research in Texas Archaeology, 5:00pm Saturday, Permian)

Steve Ahr (URS/AECOM)

Well-dated alluvial chronologies have been developed for many large streams within the Edwards Plateau and Gulf Coastal Plain regions of Texas. An increasingly robust database is also beginning to emerge for lower-order tributaries that occupy relatively small (<150 square km) drainage basins. Adding to this growing dataset, URS recently conducted geomorphological and geoarcheological investigations along Walnut Creek, located in south Austin. The alluvial history and geoarcheological potential of the study area was reconstructed through radiocarbon dating, detailed field recording of the alluvial pedology, and observations of cultural materials. Investigations revealed deep (6-m) and rapidly-buried archeological deposits within a complex succession of Holocene-age alluvial fills. The results of this study underscore the excellent site potential and preservation conditions that can exist in smaller stream settings.

Artifacts from the 1847 Kellum Noble House in Houston Provide a Glimpse of Its Illustrious Past (Paper, Texas Archeological Stewards Network Symposium, 3:00pm Friday, Paluxy)

Beth Aucoin (Texas Archeological Stewards Network)

Built between March 1847 and February 1848, the Kellum Noble House is the oldest known building in Houston still standing and is the only structure in Sam Houston Park on its original site. During recent foundation stabilization work in December 2014 an impressive assemblage of artifacts began to emerge. The finding of those artifacts prompted the Texas Historical Commission's request to the Houston Archeological Society to spearhead an emergency salvage archeology project. Two days later, 50 members were on-site to begin the meticulous screening of tons of earth that had been removed from beneath the floors of the house. Artifacts recovered included pieces of an ironstone chamber pot, a pristine ink well, slate pencils and slate with traces of letters upon it, still unidentified transfer ware and exotic china, gorgeous and rare china marbles imported from Germany, a tea pot lid, an English shell-pattern sterling fork, and a selection of pipes including an effigy pipe. The project that ended in late February 2015 resulted in the recovery of 10,200+ artifacts—artifacts that shed light on the history of the house and its inhabitants.

B

Oh the Weather Outside was Frightful, but the ~~Margarita~~ Company was so Delightful: A Report on the 2015 TAS Field School (Paper, General Session – TAS Field School, 11:20am Saturday, Permian)

Jason W. Barrett (Texas Department of Transportation)

The Texas Archeological Society returned in 2015 to the Tait-Huffmeyer Ranch in Columbus, TX for a second field season. Investigations this summer focused on expanding upon previous excavations at two of the historic sites and one of the prehistoric sites that were initially explored during the 2014 TAS-FS. While some progress and several interesting new discoveries were made, one uninvited guest – Tropical Storm Bill – camped out with us for much of the week, limiting what we were ultimately able to accomplish. The weather conditions eventually necessitated having to call an early end to the Field School as access roads on the ranch became inundated and soils at each of the sites became waterlogged and impossible to excavate. This paper highlights some of the significant findings from the work that was completed this past summer. It also presents an overview of project's findings to date and discus the ongoing plans for continued excavations at the Cotton Field (41CD155) and Bluff (41CD124) sites. Members of the TAS, regional archaeological societies, and students in Anthropology programs across the state are invited to help investigate these fascinating sites and explore important, transitional periods in Texas history.

Vandalism and Property Destruction in the 21st Century: Understanding the Challenges of Researching an Historic Cemetery in North Central Texas (Paper, General Session – Archaeology of the Historic Period in Texas, 11:00am Saturday, Paluxy)

Chris Barry (Tarrant County Archeological Society) and Catrina Whitley (Tarrant County Archeological Society)

The Johnson Plantation Cemetery is an historic cemetery situated in Arlington, Texas within Tarrant County and contains graves from the mid-19th century through the mid-20th century. The cemetery includes the grave of Col. Middleton Tate Johnson. Col. Johnson, considered the father of Tarrant County and for whom Johnson County is named, was a wealthy landowner prior to the Civil War and known to be the largest owner of slaves in Tarrant County. The Col. Middleton Tate Johnson Plantation cemetery is located in a major urban area and development over the last half century has resulted in encroachment of modern streets, businesses, and housing. As a result, the cemetery is falling into disrepair along with property destruction in the form of broken or moved headstones, sections of fencing removed, and large amounts of trash on the cemetery grounds. The Tarrant County Archeological Society Johnson Station Plantation Research Project focuses on researching the family lineages of those buried, identification of potentially unrecorded individuals, identifying the location of unmarked graves, and establishing the boundaries of the cemetery using survey and ground penetrating radar. This talk will discuss the problems associated with researching a historic cemetery in the midst of active destruction.

Processing Acorns: "There is nothing to it" (Paper, Barnhill Rockshelter Symposium, 10:40am Saturday, Permian)

Gracie Beard (Baylor University) and Krissa Green (Baylor University)

Carbonized shells of pecans, walnuts and acorns have been recovered from thermal features and middens at Barnhill Rockshelter #3 (41CV1646). Pecans and walnuts are commonly used in modern American cuisine, but acorns are not. However, they were a dietary staple for many prehistoric Native Americans, including the hunters and gatherers residing on the Edwards Plateau. In order to better understand the process of preparing acorns for consumption, we carried out an experiment in processing acorns. This presentation chronicles our experiment. We started with eight pounds of acorns and ended with two-thirds of a pound of acorn flour. Following a Native

Californian recipe, we cooked our acorn cakes on a griddle. We spent 29 hours on this experiment and it was well worth the effort.

Macrobotanical Analysis of the Carbonized Plant Remains Recovered from Three Earth Ovens and a Midden at Barnhill Rockshelter #3 (41VC1646), Coryell County, Texas (Paper, Barnhill Rockshelter Symposium, 10:20am Saturday, Permian)

Nicole Beckwith (Baylor University) and Leslie Bush (Macrobotanical Analysis)

During the 2015 Baylor University Archaeological Field School at Barnhill Rockshelter #3 (41CV1646), two earth ovens and a midden were encountered, resting on the bedrock surface of the rockshelter. Diagnostic artifacts recovered from these features date them to the Austin Phase of the Late Prehistoric Period. This presentation will first describe the context of these features as well as that of an earth oven encountered in 2013; second, discuss the macrobotanical remains recovered from these features; and third, present the results of a comparative study of the contents of these features.

Paleofeces at Eagle Cave: Preliminary Report of Ongoing Research (Poster, Eagle Nest Canyon Session, Saturday 11:00am-3:00pm, Texas Ballroom Foyer)

Stephen L. Black (Texas State University), Emily R. McCuistion (Denali National Park), Matthew E. Larsen (Lower Colorado River Authority), and Chase W. Beck (Texas A&M University)

The 2015 Ancient Southwest Texas Project excavation in Eagle Cave (41VV167) was the first to document paleofeces (coprolites) at the site. Though the site was partially excavated in the 1930s and 1960s, studies of paleofeces were uncommon until the 1970s. This poster presents observations about depositional context and spatial distribution, weight, color, and form of the Eagle Cave paleofeces, and some preliminary assessments of visible macrobotanical and faunal remains. Also presented is an overview of excavation and handling methods. As is typical of dry rockshelter sites in the Lower Pecos Canyonlands, preservation in Eagle Cave is excellent overall. However, as preservation quality varies across the site, the relationship of these fragile remains to site preservation is also presented here. Initial results from a pilot analytic project are presented to highlight avenues of future analysis including macrofossils, pollen, phytoliths, parasites, DNA, radiocarbon dating, and comparison studies with paleofeces from other sites, such as Hinds Cave.

The Rock Art and the History of San Esteban Rockshelter, Presidio County, Texas (Paper, Big Bend Archeology Symposium, 4:50pm Saturday, Paluxy)

Roger Boren (Center for Big Bend Studies, Sul Ross State University)

San Esteban rockshelter is located in the Alamito Creek basin in Presidio County, Texas. This drainage formerly constituted a portion of the old Salt Trail and later the historic Chihuahua Trail which extended from Indianola, Texas on the Gulf Coast to Chihuahua City, Chihuahua, Mexico. San Esteban rockshelter provides a permanent source of water as well as shelter from the elements. Through time visitors have carved and painted many designs on the shelter's walls. This rock art was noted as early as 1909 when Charles Peabody traveled through the drainage. The. Center for Big Bend Studies in conjunction with the Texas Archeological Society conducted a field school at San Esteban rockshelter in 2000. This presentation discusses the rock art at San Esteban rockshelter and takes a look at some of its history.

A GIS Analysis of Alibates Quarries and Antelope Creek Sites - An Update (Paper, General Session – New Methods and Research in Texas Archaeology, 2:20pm Saturday, Permian)

Britt Bousman (Texas State University), Virginia Moore (Atkins), and Bob Wishoff (Brenham Heritage Museum)

The spatial analysis of the Alibates Quarries, and related sites in relation to surrounding Antelope Creek sites provides a model of quarry behavior and raw material access that has been unavailable with more traditional forms of analysis. The construction of cost-surfaces based on topography and known hazards allows for the estimation of paths between sites based on walk-time offering a different and more realistic method to evaluate spatial relationships. New maps have been generated providing a unique view on the acquisition and distribution of lithic materials from the Alibates Quarries to Antelope Creek sites in the Panhandle.

Don't Forget the Garbage! Documenting Urban Trash Dumps as Evidence of Municipal Waste Management Practices and Socioeconomic Discrimination (Paper, General Session – Archaeology of the Houston Area, 8:40am Saturday, Paluxy)

Douglas K. Boyd (Prewitt and Associates, Inc.)

Large deposits of trash in urban settings are often ignored as having little or no research value. This may be true when an individual deposit is viewed in isolation, but these sites can contribute to urban archeological research. When viewed in a broader geographic, temporal, and socioeconomic contexts, such deposits reflect the evolution of waste management policies in any given city. Recent and past findings of large deposits of incinerated trash fill in Houston are described as an example. The placement of incinerated trash deposits, and the placement of the trash incinerators themselves, was not random in Houston. Historical and archeological evidence indicates that municipal garbage incinerators, and the dumps of burned garbage they produced, were concentrated in lower income, predominantly African American and Hispanic neighborhoods. In order for these types of sites to provide useful data, a basic and consistent level of archeological documentation is suggested for urban trash dumps.

Botanical preservation in Texas Rockshelters: Eagle Nest Canyon (northeastern Chihuahuan Desert) and McCutchen Branch (Lampasas Cut Plain) (Poster, Eagle Nest Canyon Session, Saturday 11:00am-3:00pm, Texas Ballroom Foyer)

Leslie L. Bush (Macrobotanical Analysis), Kevin Hanselka (Texas Department of Transportation), Christina M. Nielsen (Texas State University), Daniel Rodriguez (Texas State University), and Carol A. Macaulay-Jameson (Baylor University)

Analysis of botanical samples from rockshelter sites in two different ecological areas of Texas highlight the exceptional value of such sites for paleoethnobotanical research but also the complexities of botanical preservation within and between shelters. In Eagle Nest Canyon, a tributary of the Rio Grande River in the northeastern Chihuahuan Desert, delicate and uncarbonized plant parts such as lechuguilla fibers and bristlegrass chaff are preserved along with the tough, carbonized plant parts that are typically found on open air sites in the area. Preservation does not follow a simple, improving gradient of preservation from the front to the back of the shelters, however. In the more humid climate of central Texas, ancient plant remains at the Barnhill #3 Site (41CV1646) are completely carbonized, or nearly so. Although uncarbonized plant parts are not preserved, the rock shelter provides conditions for the preservation of delicate plant parts such as grass stems and wind-dispersed seeds that are rare to absent on open air sites in the region.

C

Rock Imagery on the Pinto Canyon Ranch (Poster, Saturday 8:30am-10:30am, Texas Ballroom Foyer)

Samuel S. Cason (Center for Big Bend Studies, Sul Ross State University)

The Pinto Canyon Ranch is located in a remote portion of Big Bend country along the Texas side of the Rio Grande borderlands. Rock imagery is one of the most striking aspects of archaeology in this rugged setting, due in large part to the staggering diversity of methods, subject matter, and—we speculate—time. Represented in roughly 15 years of documentation are pictographs, petroglyphs, abraded lines, cupules, and stone arrangements. Among the various representations are abstract geometric designs, anthropomorphs, zoomorphs, fertility symbols, hunting tableaus, and super complex linear mosaics. One recently discovered pattern is petroglyphs on basalt boulders that depict a variety of themes, including aboriginal horse nomad iconography amidst livestock brands. This poster presents a survey of the various images discovered across the ranch.

Archaeological Research on the Pinto Canyon Ranch, Presidio County, Texas (Paper, Big Bend Archeology Symposium, 4:30pm Saturday, Paluxy)

Samuel S. Cason (Center for Big Bend Studies, Sul Ross State University)

The Pinto Canyon Ranch is located in a remote portion of Big Bend country along the Texas side of the Rio Grande borderlands. Totaling more than 63,000 acres, the ranch is the backdrop of dramatic cultural developments—both prehistoric and historic—amidst a complex and wild geographic setting. Cultural chronologies and a better understanding of behavioral diversity are coming to light as a result of investigations carried out by Center for Big Bend Studies, part of Sul Ross State University in Alpine. This presentation provides an overview of CBBS research as well as the characteristics of prehistoric archaeology on the PCR including rock art, thermal appliances, structural remnants, special use features, and artifact scatters.

Texas State University 2015 Field School Investigations at Horse Trail Shelter (Poster, Eagle Nest Canyon Session, Saturday 11:00am-3:00pm, Texas Ballroom Foyer)

Amanda Castañeda (Texas State University); Charles Koenig (Texas State University)

The 2015 Texas State University Lower Pecos Canyonlands Archaeological Field School undertook excavations at Horse Trail Shelter, a long, narrow overhang located on the western wall of Eagle Nest Canyon. Besides a few shovel tests and small units excavated by the ASWT project during the 2014 field season, no other archaeological investigations had taken place at Horse Trail. Over the course of the field school we investigated several different areas across the site. Two excavation areas were placed near boulders with grinding features, a trench was excavated from the back wall out to the talus slope through the greatest density of burned rock, and we fully exposed an intriguing pit feature that was originally uncovered in 2014 at the south end of the site. This poster provides a summary of our fieldwork and points to avenues for future comparisons with other rockshelters in Eagle Nest Canyon and beyond.

The Genevieve Lykes Duncan Site: A Late Paleoindian Campsite in the Chihuahuan Desert (Paper, Big Bend Archeology Symposium, 3:30pm Saturday, Paluxy)

William A. "Andy" Cloud, (Center for Big Bend Studies, Sul Ross State University), Richard W. Walter (Center for Big Bend Studies, Sul Ross State University)

Archaeologists have been searching for Paleoindian sites in the greater Big Bend region for decades, but with little success. However, discovery several years ago of deeply buried Late Paleoindian components at the Genevieve Lykes Duncan (GLD) site on the 02 Ranch, opened the door to insightful research of some of the early inhabitants and ancient environments of the region. Remarkably intact features with abundant charcoal have yielded a series of radiocarbon assays indicating occupations at the site began as early as ca. 11,000 years ago. This presentation highlights findings from Center for Big Bend Studies research of the site.

Using Ethnographies to Interpret the Spatial Patterning at Barnhill Rockshelter #3 (Paper, Barnhill Rockshelter Symposium, 8:40am Saturday, Permian)

William Crisp (Baylor University)

This presentation will examine four ethnoarchaeological projects conducted over the last 50 years in Tanzania, Namibia, South Africa and Australia, with a focus on how hunters and gatherers utilized the space within 16 rockshelters, specifically looking at hearths, sleeping areas and refuse disposal areas. Based on these studies, a representational model of activity zones is presented and provides a framework regarding the use of space within rockshelters. The spatial layout of Barnhill Rockshelter #3 will be assessed within this model, in order to see if similar patterns appear within its spatial confines and if these patterns transcend the occupational periods of the rockshelter.

The Timber Fawn Clovis Site, Kingwood, Harris County, Texas (Paper, General Session – Perspectives on the Paleoindian and Archaic Periods in Texas, 9:00am Saturday, Woodbine)

Wilson W. "Dub" Crook, III (Houston Archeological Society); Lenore A. Psencik (Houston Archeological Society); Linda C. Gorski (Houston Archeological Society); Thomas L. Nuckols (Houston Archeological Society)

In November, 2014 HAS member Lenore Psencik discovered a distinctive Clovis blade at the new Rivergrove housing development in Kingwood, Harris County, Texas. Permission to conduct a surface survey of the area prior to house construction was obtained from the developer, KB Home. Investigations at the site have recovered a total of 24 tools of apparent Clovis affinity among which are two Clovis points, two bifaces, parts of 8 blades, three unifacial end-scrapers, an adze, six worked flakes, a single small well-used hammerstone, and part of an engraved quartzite gorget. Measurement of the blades on a triangular configuration diagram shows they have a close affinity to similar blades from Gault (41BL323), Keven Davis (41NV659) and other Texas Clovis contexts. Many of the artifacts have the same coloration and UV response as chert from known Central Texas Clovis locations such as the Gault site. To test the possibility of interaction between the aboriginal inhabitants of Timber Fawn and Central Texas, all of the chert artifacts have been subjected to trace element geochemical analysis using X-Ray Fluorescence (XRF). This presentation summarizes the results of our analytical study and discusses the implications for Clovis toolstone procurement and mobility across Texas.

D

Finding the 370th: The Archaeology of a World War I Training Camp in Houston, Texas (Poster, Saturday 8:30am-10:30am, Texas Ballroom Foyer)

Dylan Dickens (Rice University), Rachel George (Rice University), Jake Krauss (Rice University), Jeffrey Fleisher (Rice University)

This research project aims to explore the experiences of African-American soldiers in a World War I training camp during a time of heightened racial tensions. The 370th U.S. Infantry was a segregated regiment of black soldiers brought to train in Camp Logan, in Houston, Texas, not only during the repressive era of Jim Crow segregation, but also just months after Houston's only race riot in 1917. The work reported here focuses on archaeological research at the Camp Logan site in Memorial Park in Houston, which was aimed at determining its viability as a research site for future historical archaeology of the 370th's time at Camp Logan.

X-ray Fluorescence Analysis of Rock Art in Big Bend Ranch State Park, Presidio and Brewster Counties, Texas (Paper, General Session – New Methods in Rock Art Research, 11:40am Saturday, Woodbine)

Christopher Dostal (Texas A&M University) and Morgan Smith (Texas A&M University)

In April 2015, researchers from Texas A&M University's Anthropology Department collaborated with Texas Parks and Wildlife Department archaeologists to use portable X-ray fluorescence (pXRF) to determine the primary elemental composition of Native American and potentially European rock art in Big Bend Ranch State Park, Presidio and Brewster counties, Texas. Variations in the pigment compositions in the Native American rock art appear to correspond with stylistic differences, allowing a degree of quantitative validity in the definition of separate styles. Further, the identification of elements and minerals responsible for primary rock art pigments (notably red, orange, white, and black) provides some insight into raw material acquisition used for early art. The following paper will outline the methodology for sampling and analysis, the results of the analysis, and discuss the strengths and weaknesses of pXRF for this type of study.

Skeletal Pathologies of Prehistoric Individuals at Falcon Reservoir (Paper, TARL Today Symposium, 2:10pm Saturday, Paluxy)

Stacy M. Drake

As lake levels dropped significantly in the 1990s, numerous archaeological sites were exposed within the Falcon Reservoir along the Rio Grande River in southern Texas. Many of these newly exposed sites contained human burials, some of which were excavated or looted by collectors. In the hopes of protecting these sites from rampant cultural and environmental destruction, a long-term effort was set about in 1995 to record exposed sites within the Falcon Reservoir area. In June of 2014, the Texas Archeological Research Laboratory (TARL) was asked by the International Boundary and Water Commission (IBWC) to revisit these burials under a NAGPRA grant. This paper will address the results of the most recent osteological analysis of approximately 33 bodies exhumed during the Falcon Reservoir salvage project of the 1990s. Particular focus will be placed on the pathological conditions exhibited by the remains, with the intention to illustrate common physical and health conditions experienced by the prehistoric populations of Zapata County, Texas and northern Tamaulipas, Mexico.

F

Cotton Field in Context: Some Preliminary Observations on the Site and Its Setting (Paper, General Session – TAS Field School, 11:40am Saturday, Permian)

Charles D. Frederick (Geoarchaeological Consultant, Dublin, Texas)

Prior to the start of the field school the deposits exposed by last year's excavation were examined in order to assess the context and integrity of the prehistoric occupations present. This paper presents a preliminary look at the site, its setting and how these deposits fit into the previously established Colorado River alluvial stratigraphic sequence.

The Late Quaternary Stratigraphic Setting of Genevieve Lykes-Duncan Site, O2 Ranch, Brewster County, Texas (Paper, Big Bend Archeology Symposium, 3:50pm Saturday, Paluxy)

Charles D. Frederick (Geoarchaeological Consultant, Dublin Texas), Brittney Gregory (Louisiana State University), David Yelacic (Texas State University)

The discovery of the Genevieve Lykes-Duncan was the result of a methodical search mounted by the Center for Big Bend Studies for buried Paleoindian sites in context. Late Quaternary deposits that could that could be of Paleoindian age were identified using soil-geomorphic criteria based upon the work of Claude Albritton, Kirk Bryanand J. Charles Kelley in the late 1930's. Scrutiny of many such deposits over a number of years eventually led to a locality near Terlingua Creek on the O2 Ranch. This paper discusses how the site was found and provides a basic overview of its stratigraphic context.

G

Con un pie en cada lado: Nuevo Santander Ranching Communities (Paper, Trans Rio Bravo/Rio Grande International Research Collaboration Symposium, 3:10pm Saturday, Woodbine)

Mary Jo Galindo (Atkins)

Before the Río Grande valley became a contested border between the United States and Mexico, and between predominantly Latino and Anglo- American societies, it was the northern frontier of Spanish Nuevo Santander and a border between Spanish Mexico and indigenous societies to the north. Between 1748 and 1755, the civilian colonists of Nuevo Santander established 23 communities, including 6 along the banks of the Río Grande. The pobladores, or colonists, and their descendants had to adapt constantly to the changing political, economic, and social environment, as people in borderlands always do. These pobladores received porciones, or land grants, on both banks of the river, and they and their descendants literally lived con un pie en cada lado, with a foot on each side of the Río Grande. Thus, these ranches were among the first of their kind in present-day Texas, representing a unique form of civilian colonization based on the relocation of entire families, and without major emphasis on missions or presidios. Descendants of these colonists in the Lower Rio Grande Valley still maintain connections to the land and artifacts from their ranches have been used in recent years to teach school-age children about the local history.

Search for the Twin Sisters Cannons (Paper, General Session – Archaeology of the Houston Area, 8:00am Saturday, Paluxy)

Jorge Garcia-Herreros (Gulf Coast Archaeology Group), Jasmin Talbert (PGCS)

The Twin Sisters are cannons which were one of the principal weapons used in the Battle of San Jacinto. After their crucial role in this battle they became symbols of the victory of Texas over Mexico. During the Civil War, the cannons again saw service in the Battle of Galveston. After the Civil War, the cannons disappeared. A story that arose was that Dr. Henry North Graves had buried the cannons in Harrisburg in order to prevent the Union from taking them. Since then multiple attempts have been made to find these cannons. In 2011, a non-profit group was created to perform a comprehensive search for the infamous cannons. This search was based on a newly developed hypothesis as to the location of the cannons. To locate areas of interest a cesium vapor magnetometer survey was conducted. The data gathered was processed in order to delineate the cannons and other buried artifacts. This paper describes the search that was conducted for the cannons and its findings.

Life along the Brazos: Testing at a Possible Tenant Home near Richmond, Texas (Poster, Saturday 8:30am-10:30am, Texas Ballroom Foyer)

Anastasia Gilmer (Moore Archeological Consulting, Inc.) and John R. Ferguson (Moore Archeological Consulting, Inc.)

Site 41FB346 is a small historic occupation recorded during a 2015 survey and further investigated during testing by Moore Archeological Consulting, Inc. The site, located near Richmond, Texas, is located 150 m to the northeast of the Lamar-Calder House. The construction of the Lamar-Calder House was completed by Mirabeau Lamar's widow, Henrietta Lamar, for their daughter, Loretto, and her husband, Samuel Calder in 1861. A well and a small brick pavement -- both constructed from hand-made, low-fired brick -- were noted during the pedestrian survey. Shovel testing and backhoe work revealed a subsurface brick pavement -- also constructed from hand-made, low-fired brick -- to the north and east of the well. This un-mortared pavement probably represents a brick-paved interior of a wooded structure, rather than a brick-paved walkway. The early low-fired bricks initially suggested these features pre-dated 1870; however, it seems these bricks were repurposed for a late 19th century structure given the presence of late 19th century domestic artifacts, and that the brick pavement was not mortared yet mortar was present on the brick faces. This structure appears to be the home of a tenant or servant who was associated with an important family in Texas's early history.

Ghosts on the Mudflats: Artifacts from the Lost Townsite of San Jacinto (Paper, Texas Archeological Stewards Network Symposium, 4:00pm Friday, Paluxy)

Linda Gorski (Texas Archeological Stewards Network and President, Houston Archeological Society) and Larry Golden (Houston Archeological Society)

Artifacts recovered from the mudflats on Buffalo Bayou near the forgotten 1820s - 1900 Townsite of San Jacinto are prompting new archeological investigations in the area. Collected during very low tides caused by "blue northers" in the 1960s by the Golden family of Pasadena, these artifacts, currently being researched and catalogued by the Houston Archeological Society, give us a unique glimpse of life in Texas before, during and after the Texas revolution. The Townsite adjoined the San Jacinto Battlefield and many of the artifacts date to the 1836 period of the Battle. The townsite was also a gathering site for Texians fleeing during the Runaway Scrape in 1836 as well as the site of an important Civil War armory in the 1860s. Among the items in this large and important collection are coins dating from 1829 to 1900, buttons from Mexican and Texian military uniforms, military buckles, munitions and a number of remarkable clay pipe bowls, including presidential effigy pipes. The ceramics, glassware, bottles, stoneware jugs and children's marbles and toys show us that families lived and thrived there, too. The collection of trade beads recovered at the site indicate even earlier occupation – perhaps to French explorers in the 1700s.

How a Collection becomes a TAS Field School (Paper, Texas Archeological Stewards Network Symposium, 3:40pm Friday, Paluxy)

W. Sue Gross (Brazosport Archaeological Society)

There are many different resources to help an avocational recognize, identify, and record an archeological site. These sites can vary from pre-historic camp site, lithic scatter, midden, to historic occupation. What do you do when a landowner's extensive collection contains all of these elements? This discussion will be from an avocational and personal perspective to document and submit the site(s) as a potential area of interest for a TAS Field School (Columbus 2014-2015).

Preliminary Results of an Archaeological Survey in Eastern Brewster County (Paper, General Session – Perspectives on the Paleoindian and Archaic Periods in Texas, 8:00am Saturday, Woodbine)

Caitlin Gulihur (Texas State University)

In July and August 2015, a 6 week pedestrian survey inspected nearly 1,000 acres in eastern Brewster County in order to better understand the settlement patterns of the region. The survey was designed to study how rockshelters affect the location of open campsites on the landscape. Thirty-four sites were found. The sites ranged from large, well-used rockshelters to light lithic scatters and dated from the Middle Archaic to the Late Prehistoric. This paper details the methods and preliminary results from that survey, as well as the difficulties inherent in trying to locate and identify previously recorded sites in this region.

H

A Search for the Henderson Yoakum House Using Historical Documents and Geophysical Survey (Poster, Saturday 8:30am-10:30am, Texas Ballroom Foyer)

Bryan S. Haley (Coastal Environments Inc.) and Douglas G. Mangum (Moore Archaeological Consulting)

Henderson Yoakum was a prominent historian, lawyer, and military officer, and seminal 19th century figure in Walker County and Texas as a whole. In 1855, at the request of Sam Houston, who was a close friend and associate, Yoakum wrote the first history of Texas from his home located east of Huntsville. This project examines historical documents, georeferenced maps and aerial photographs, and geophysical data produced with a Foerster Ferex fluxgate gradiometer in order to locate features associated with the Yoakum House. Magnetic gradiometer anomalies were related to specific features through targeted excavations.

Preliminary Ecologically Diagnostic Xylem Analysis (EDXA) of Mesquite Wood along an East-West Transect Across Texas, and Implications for Ancient Rainfall Patterns (Paper, General Session – New Methods and Research in Texas Archaeology, 3:00pm Saturday, Permian)

Kevin Hanselka (Texas Department of Transportation)

Ecologically Diagnostic Xylem Analysis (EDXA) is based on the principle that wood anatomy can vary within the basic pattern of a species in response to environmental conditions. Studies in South Africa have shown that some tree species exhibit predictable variation in diameter and density of water transport vessels in their wood depending on local rainfall regimes: with increasing rainfall, vessel diameter increases and vessel density decreases. Dr. Phil Dering recently pioneered application of EDXA on mesquite (Prosopis glandulosa) to Texas archeology. In theory, the general moisture regime in effect during the growth cycle of archeologically derived mesquite can be inferred from a morphometric baseline established from experimentally burned modern wood grown under known moisture conditions. Expanding on this research with support from the Texas Department of Transportation, I am accumulating for EDXA modern mesquite wood from widely dispersed areas and settings across Texas. Here I present results for 25 modern mesquite wood samples along an east-west transect across the state compared against the general precipitation gradient along the same axis. The goal of this ongoing study is to build a proxy baseline dataset for interpreting ancient precipitation regimes in Texas using archaeological mesquite wood charcoal.

Rethinking Archaeological Field Forms: The Use and Application of Mobile Computing to Collect Archaeological Data (Paper, General Session – New Methods and Research in Texas Archaeology, 4:20pm Saturday, Permian)

Christian Hartnett (SWCA Environmental Consultants)

With the ubiquity of mobile computing devices such as smart phones and tablet computers, there has been an increased interest in the use of these devices to collect archaeological data in the field. Over the past year, the Austin and San Antonio offices of SWCA Environmental Consultants (SWCA) have gone through the process of developing, testing, and fielding a series of digital archaeological forms. The aim of this paper will be to outline the complex developmental cycle of mobile data collection for archaeological applications. Using examples drawn from several recent SWCA archaeological surveys, specific attention will be given to describing best practices for developing usable forms, how the data is aggregated and utilized by a database, and the advantages and disadvantages of collecting data digitally.

Eagle Cave South Trench 2015: Cleaning the Kitchen at Feature 8 (Poster, Eagle Nest Canyon Session, Saturday 11:00am-3:00pm, Texas Ballroom Foyer)

Bryan Heisinger (Sequoia and Kings Canyon National Parks)

During the 2015 ASWT ENC Expedition, the crew uncovered and sampled Feature 8 - a centrally located heating element complex near the back of Eagle Cave. Feature 8 showed characteristically representative examples of continuous earth oven baking. Further, many of the limestone rocks were large (11-15 cm) in size and inclined at the base of the pit. The soil that surrounded these fire-cracked rocks (FCR) was heavily organic, ashy, rich with dime-size charcoal chunks, and almost entirely absent of artifacts. In profile, Feature 8 aids in our understanding of the larger structural patterning and formation processes within Eagle Cave's deposits. However, its attributes contrast in many ways to the other south trench profile sections that were uncovered during the 2015 field season. This poster provides a preliminary summary of the data recovered from Feature 8.

50 Years along the Rio Grande: Reflections on a Variety of Archaeological Research Projects on the Border (Paper, Trans Rio Bravo/Rio Grande International Research Collaboration Symposium, 1:30pm Saturday, Woodbine)

Thomas R. Hester (Professor of Anthropology Emeritus, The University of Texas at Austin)

For 50 years, I have taken part in numerous of archaeological studies along the middle and upper Rio Grande. I briefly review a number of these here, with emphasis on those that have involved participation of colleagues in Mexico. These activities began, unfortunately, with digging into Rio Grande rockshelters while in high school! After enrolling at UT-Austin, the focus of fieldwork shifted. In 1967, I was involved in the salvage of Mexican War dead, a saga that continued many years and involved the public and the Mexican government. In the 1970s, I helped conduct extensive excavations at the Spanish missions at Guerrero, Mexico. Later, students and I recorded a rock art site rare on the middle Rio Grande. In the 1970s-1990s, I worked with collectors and avocationals on both sides of the border to document and help them publish important finds. During this period and up to today, I conducted obsidian sourcing studies involving the lower Rio Grande. In 1995, I was part of a large team recording the damage to Falcon Reservoir sites during a serious drought. Also in the 1990s, I worked on a project involving the illegal importation of Mexican artifacts, culminating in a major conference and exhibit in Laredo. Through these projects, I have learned much about the border and interaction with colleagues on both sides of the Rio Grande.

Use and Delineation of Space within Barnhill Rockshelter #3 (Paper, Barnhill Rockshelter Symposium, 9:00am Saturday, Permian)

Cassady Holt (Baylor University)

Barnhill Rockshelter #3 (41CV1646) is a large rockshelter that was occupied by hunting and gathering groups residing in central Texas during the Late Prehistoric period. This presentation examines the use and delineation of space within the rockshelter. First, the anatomy of the rockshelter is described and how it structured the occupants' use of space is proposed. Second, by using Spatial Analyst tools in ArcMap; areas within the rockshelter where retooling, animal carcass processing, and stone boiling; are located. And third, a discussion as to why these areas were chosen for these specific activities is presented.

J

The Legacy of A.T. Jackson (Paper, TARL Today Symposium, 1:30pm Saturday, Paluxy)

Jonathan Jarvis (Texas Archeological Research Lab)

Archeological projects conducted by the University of Texas under the auspices of the Works Projects Administration (WPA) greatly advanced our understanding of Texas' prehistory and formed the basis of a collection and archive that would eventually become the Texas Archeological Research Laboratory. Although our methods and research questions have evolved since that time, we are still very much indebted to WPA archeology. This presentation will briefly examine the extraordinary legacy of A.T. Jackson, one of the leaders of the WPA's field efforts in Texas.

Extending Arenosa Shelter's Reach: Zooarchaeological Research in Eagle Nest Canyon 2015 (Poster, Eagle Nest Canyon Session, Saturday 11:00am-3:00pm, Texas Ballroom Foyer)

Christopher Jurgens (Texas State University); Haley Rush (Cox/McClain Environmental Consulting, Inc.)

Results of preliminary faunal analyses conducted on materials recovered at two sites in Eagle Nest Canyon (ENC) are being compared to those of previous faunal analyses by Jurgens (2005) from Arenosa Shelter (41VV99) on the Pecos River. Faunal materials and bone artifacts from 2014 ENC excavations at Skiles Shelter (41VV165) and Eagle Cave (41VV167) have been analyzed using the methodology developed by Jurgens (2005). Using these ENC materials, the research conclusions and suggestions for further research posited by Jurgens (2005) have been used to examine zooarchaeological and bone technology characteristics of the faunal materials recovered in 2014 from Skiles Shelter and Eagle Cave. While the analyses are on-going, striking similarities with the Arenosa Shelter collections have been recognized in terms of species diversity, subsistence processing, and subsequent technological modifications.

K

Radiocarbon Based Occupation Patterns of the San Antonio River (Poster, Saturday 8:30am-10:30am, Texas Ballroom Foyer)

Leonard Kemp (Center for Archaeological Research-University of Texas at San Antonio), Raymond Mauldin (Center for Archaeological Research-University of Texas at San Antonio), Jason B. Perez (Center for Archaeological Research-University of Texas at San Antonio), William Unsinn (Center for Archaeological Research-University of Texas at San Antonio)

In this poster, we explore the potential of summed probability distributions from radiocarbon dates as an indicator of the intensity of use on a landscape. While our focus is on a 10-kilometer segment of the San Antonio River where CAR-UTSA has recently conducted extensive work, we used charcoal and bone dates from excavations throughout the San Antonio River Basin. We have eliminated all dates with sigmas greater than +/- 100 years, and those not directly associated with human groups. In addition, we averaged multiple dates from a given feature where that was statistically appropriate. Our resulting data set consists of roughly 320 calibrated radiocarbon dates from 40 sites in six counties, though most of the dates (ca. 300) come from Bexar County. Research interest, differential preservation, and biases introduced by the calibration curve all impact a summed probability pattern. We consider ways to reduce those impacts, and argue that the resulting pattern may provide a rough approximation of the intensity of landscape use along this section of the San Antonio River.

2015 Investigations of Eagle Cave (Poster, Eagle Nest Canyon Session, Saturday 11:00am-3:00pm, Texas Ballroom Foyer)

Charles W. Koenig (Texas State University) and Stephen L. Black (Texas State University)

The spring 2015 ASWT investigations focused exclusively on exposing, documenting, and sampling the south wall of the main trench at Eagle Cave. In 2014 the work in Eagle Cave focused on creating several small exposures to test our recording and excavation methods. In 2015 we were able to use the lessons learned in 2014 to begin fully exposing the south wall. This poster provides a brief overview of previous ENC investigations, describes the 2015 work in Eagle Cave, and offers some preliminary findings and interpretations of the Eagle Cave deposits.

Beyond the Square Hole: Application of Structure from Motion Photogrammetry to Archaeological Excavation (Paper, 3D Data in Archaeology Symposium, 4:00pm Friday, Woodbine)

Charles W. Koenig (Texas State University), Mark D. Willis (Blanton and Associates), Stephen L. Black (Texas State University)

When conducting archaeological excavations, two of the most important pieces of information we record are the context and provenience of everything from artifacts to sites. For decades the standard procedures for how we collect this data has remained largely unchanged (e.g., 1-x-1 meter units excavated in 10 centimeter levels). Recently the use of Structure from Motion (SfM) photogrammetry is becoming more widespread for producing 3D maps and orthophotos of archaeological sites and features. We argue SfM is not just a tool useful for mapping sites and architecture. SfM allows archaeologists to collect precise 3D data at the scale of the excavation unit and profile. As part of the Ancient Southwest Texas project, we are using ground-based SfM as the basic documentation method for excavation units and profiles during our work in the Lower Pecos. Using ground-based SfM, we maintain 3D provenience on all excavation units, layers, and profiles without rigorously maintaining a "grid" and excavating square holes in arbitrary levels. Further, this method allows the archaeology to guide our excavation strategy (and subsequent recovery of artifacts and samples) – something difficult to do using traditional methods. This presentation demonstrates the usefulness of ground-based SfM photogrammetry in lieu of traditional square-hole methodology.

L

Eagle Cave South Trench 2015: Initial Results from Profile Section 9 (Poster, Eagle Nest Canyon Session, Saturday 11:00am-3:00pm, Texas Ballroom Foyer)

Matthew E. Larsen (Lower Colorado River Authority)

Profile Section 009 (PS009) is a complexly stratified north-south profile exposed during the 2015 field season. PS009 is a very interesting profile exposure for several reasons. It is one of the only profile exposures perpendicular to the excavation trench and, therefore, provides a different perspective than the many other exposed profile sections. The composition of PS009 is interesting, as it constitutes some 28 defined strata, nearly double those of the average profile section, and is mostly comprised of alternating ashy, fibrous, and charcoal-rich material. Additionally, the assemblage of artifacts recovered from this profile differs significantly from other units and profile sections towards the dripline, providing some clues as to the differing activity zones within the rockshelter. This poster presents an overview of PS009. It will briefly explain the recording and sampling methodology. It will describe the profile and the strata, as well as the artifact assemblage. Finally, it will present preliminary interpretations of PS009 and how it fits into the narrative of the excavation trench.

Recent Excavations at Knibbe Ranch (41CM363): Looking for a Bison Cliff Jump in Central Texas (Paper, General Session – Perspectives on the Paleoindian and Archaic Periods in Texas, 8:20am Saturday, Woodbine)

Robert Lassen (Prehistory Research Project, Texas State University)

Knibbe Ranch, established in 1852, is a Century Heritage Ranch located in the town of Spring Branch in Comal County, about 28 miles north of San Antonio. The ranch property encompasses multiple prehistoric archaeological sites. Most of these sites are made up of Archaic burned rock middens, with diagnostic artifacts ranging from

Late Paleoindian to Late Prehistoric in age. Previous excavations by the Center for Archaeological Studies encountered intact Toyah and Montell components along with significant quantities of butchered and processed bison bone in a stream valley adjacent to a ~20 foot high cliff. The geographic layout of the landscape and the archaeological presence of bison suggest that the cliff was likely used as a bison jump. The latest excavation, conducted by the Prehistory Research Project at Texas State University, consists of a 1x4 m hand excavated test trench in the talus slope at the base of the cliff. The excavation has proven logistically difficult and has not yielded substantial bison remains, so additional methods for surveying the remainder of the cliff base are being sought.

A Recalibrated Geoarchaeological Framework of Texas–Revisited (Paper, General Session –Geo-spatial Mapping and Remote Sensing, 2:00pm Friday, Woodbine)

Ken Lawrence (SWCA)

As part of research for a 2010 master's thesis, a recalibrated radiocarbon baseline was constructed and used to compare the depositional histories of select drainage basins as well as examine possible climatic influences on the drainages and, by extension, Texas archaeology.

The results of the 2010 archival study of select archaeological research projects in Texas particularly focused on alluvial deposits of Texas river basins. The research targeted projects with chronometric data from sites with deep, intact alluvial stratigraphy that encompassed the Late Pleistocene–Holocene. Subsequently, select radiocarbon assays from these previous investigations were compiled and recalibrated using the same calibration curve (i.e., INTCAL09). The uniform calibration of the radiocarbon assays provided a consistent chronological framework for all of the previous investigations that was used to compare drainage basins, paleoenvironmental data, and cultural chronologies across Texas. This paper will revisit the results of the 2010 research as well as incorporating recent chronometric data from recent archaeological projects in Texas.

A Comparison of Two Predictive Models in Abilene State Park, Taylor County, Texas (Poster, Saturday 8:30am-10:30am, Texas Ballroom Foyer)

Ken Lawrence (SWCA-Austin), Christian Hartnett (SWCA-Austin), Steve Carpenter (SWCA-Austin), Tony Lyle (TPWD), and Chris Lintz (TPWD)

Predictive models have been used in archaeology for decades, particularly for identifying high probability areas of archaeological sites for large scale investigations. This predictive modeling has systematically improved over the years with the combination of Geographic Information Systems (GIS) and more widely available spatial data, but success remains variable.

On behalf of Texas Parks and Wildlife, SWCA conducted a cultural resources survey of 789 acres of Abilene State Park (ASP) in Taylor County. These intensive investigations were guided by a simple predictive model that utilized previous investigations and physiographic factors (e.g., topography and soils). Although the predictive model was considered successful, a more robust multivariate statistical analysis developed for predicting biological species distributions using presence only data (i.e., Maximum Entropy) was subsequently applied to the data.

This poster reviews the success of the two models to determine which is more applicable for predictive modeling. Also, during the ASP field investigations an obsidian flake was encountered on a Late Prehistoric campsite (41TA107) that contained Perdiz projectile points. Analysis (XRF) was conducted on an obsidian artifact to identify a possible source for this lithic raw material. The results of the obsidian sourcing and how it compares to other regional studies are summarized.

The Harrell Site: a new perspective of Prehistoric Cemetery (Paper, TARL Today Symposium, 2:30pm Saturday, Paluxy)

Jessie LeViseur (Texas Archeological Research Lab)

The WPA excavation of the Harrell Site encountered approximately 30 individuals (some counts are 27, while the original count was 32) from the Late Prehistoric period. In conjunction with the rehabilitation of the artifact assemblage and records from this site, the human remains are currently being repackaged and reinterpreted. The original analysis of the Harrell site remains were very broad in regard to the scope of observations performed. Five of the individuals were reanalyzed twice, once in the 1960s and again in 1986, while twenty-three individuals were reanalyzed in 1986. Both analyses give basic information: gender, age at death, bone inventory and, in some instances, dentition inventories. These analyses contributed good information when they were completed but more recent bioarcheological investigations strive to provide the next observer more complete information to consider and to provide researchers of every level an overview of what each set of remains can contribute to our understanding of the impact of culture on the human skeleton. This paper will address the findings of the most recent analysis of skeletal remains from the Harrell Site through the implementation of these newer bioarchaeological insights.

Perspectives on Pictographs: Differences in Rock Art Recording Frameworks of the Rattlesnake Canyon Mural (Paper, General Session – New Methods in Rock Art Research, 11:00am Saturday, Woodbine)Audrey Kathleen Lindsay (Shumla Archaeological Research & Education Center)

Rock art documentation of complex pictograph panels includes varying recording perspectives within artistic, avocational, and professional archaeological frameworks. Analysis of different recording frameworks and methods reveals that each project captures different, yet equally important, types of information from the same rock art panel. This case study analyzes the goals, methods, and data collected from three recording projects of the Rattlesnake Canyon mural (41VV0180) in the Lower Pecos Canyonlands. The three selected projects include documentation by Forrest Kirkland, the TAS Rock Art Task Force, and the Shumla Archaeological Research & Education Center. While the three projects share a similar documentation goal, their distinct recording frameworks influenced the conception of the panel, the recording methods selected, and the types of information collected. The varied perspectives and methods applied in these documentation projects provide diverse legacy materials for the Rattlesnake Canyon panel that serve as productive resources for subsequent recorders, researchers, and land managers.

Clovis Flakes at the Gault Site... It's All in the Platform Baby! (Paper, General Session – Perspectives on the Paleoindian and Archaic Periods in Texas, 9:40am Saturday, Woodbine)

Nancy V. Littlefield (Texas State University/Gault)

Clovis biface manufacturing represents a complex reduction technology (Bradley, et al. 2010:64) and most experts agree that Clovis knappers were highly skilled in their craft. The striking platforms on Clovis flakes are reported often as being carefully prepared in order to exert control over the removal of flakes (Morrow 1995), which included mastering control of overshot flaking (Bradley 2010:466; Bradley, et al. 2010:66). However, with some exceptions (Huckell 2007; Malouf 1989; Pevny 2009), such observations are for the most part assumed, with little or no supporting data. New research has closely examined Clovis waste flakes at the Gault Site, Bell County, Texas (41BL323) that specifically focused on the prolific Clovis-age manufacturing deposits from Area 4. While no rigid patterns emerged, the data elucidate differences in the application of flake removal techniques used by Clovis knappers, thereby suggesting that Clovis knappers may have followed a system or 'template' in preparing striking platforms. This is based on trends identified in the data that highlight the application of platform preparation traits in biface-related flake types removed during reduction phases. These data have provided a greater understanding of platform preparation and flake removal techniques used to produce Clovis bifaces at the Gault Site.

The San Felipe de Austin Heritage Learning Project: Educational Partnerships and Public Archeology at the Birthplace of Texas (Paper, General Session – Archaeology of the Historic Period in Texas, 10:00am Saturday, Paluxy)

Jon C. Lohse (Coastal Environments, Inc.), Carol Salva (Spring Branch Independent School District) Brett Cruse (Texas Historical Commission)

The Texas Historical Commission is in the process of developing San Felipe de Austin, the original capital of Stephen F. Austin's colony, as a state historic site. Founded in 1824, this town played a significant role in the struggle for Texas independence from Mexico. San Felipe was the first capital of the provisional government of Texas in 1835 before it was burned to the ground following the fall of the Alamo in 1836. Coastal Environments,

Inc. is contracted to assist the THC with their multi-year plans. To maximize educational opportunities for this project, CEI and the THC have formed a collaborative partnership with Houston's Spring Branch Independent School District. This partnership brings educators into the project from the outset and allows them to design curriculum and material best suited to a wide array of learners. The objective is to enrich students' learning outcomes by centralizing their involvement and fostering a sense of co-ownership over the archeological investigative process. Participation will involve learners from several disciplines, age groups and demographic backgrounds. The nature of the project lends itself to state process, readiness and supporting standards. All lessons will be aligned with the TEKS (Texas Essentials of Knowledge and Skills) and ELPS (English Language Proficiency Standards) so that students build academic language as they deepen their learning in each subject area. This collaboration may also provide a model for educational programming involving future archeological projects.

M

A Comparative Analysis of Decorative Ceramics and Choice at the Gregory Lincoln/HSPVA Site and the Levi Jordan Plantation Site (Paper, General Session – Archaeology of the Historic Period in Texas, 10:20am Saturday, Paluxy)

Lauren Falcon Maas (SWCA Environmental Consultants)

The purpose of this research was to investigate questions of aesthetic preference or choice and other driving factors that influenced the ceramic selection by people who resided at two sites: the Gregory Lincoln/HSPVA Site in Houston, TX and the Levi Jordan Plantation Site in Brazoria County, TX as well as to compare the assemblages from these two African American sites from differing environments. These ceramics assemblages, with the exception of one context, had been previously analyzed, but a re-classification of some of the assemblages was conducted. Through a set of hypotheses, the capacity of the archaeological record to reflect the driving forces behind the consumption patterns of segments of the population at these two sites was tested. Personal preference is rarely examined in archaeological literature where the assemblages from "lower status" groups, including African Americans, are often reduced to explanations of emulation or restricted access to resources. Aesthetic preference was reflected as a consumption factor in one of the four contexts examined, and was not ruled out in the other cases. One of the significant contributions of this thesis is its suggestion that aesthetic preference and choice are indeed viable avenues of inquiry for historic archaeological sites of all populations.

Life of a Central Texas Woman 1000 Years Ago: Clues from the Archaeological Investigations at Barnhill Rockshelter #3 (41CV1646) and from Ethnohistorical Accounts (Poster, Saturday 8:30am-10:30am, Texas Ballroom Foyer)

Katie Mackenzie (Baylor University)

This poster represents the design phase of a museum exhibit depicting the life of prehistoric women, members of hunting and gathering bands, who lived in Central Texas 1000 years ago. The daily activities women would have undergone to provide food for their families is the focus of this exhibit. Four years of archaeological research conducted at Barnhill Rockshelter #3 in Coryell County, Texas as well as ethnographic accounts of European explorers provide the information depicted in this poster. To follow the women's process from harvesting to cooking, Schiffer's Consumable Product Flow Chart serves as a model to depict these activities.

Canister and Grape: Artillery related artifacts from the San Jacinto Battleground (Paper, General Session – Archaeology of the Houston Area, 9:00am Saturday, Paluxy)

Douglas Mangum (Moore Archeological Consulting, Inc.)

Over ten years of archeological investigations in and around the San Jacinto Battleground State Historic Site, Moore Archeological Consulting, Inc. recovered more than fourteen hundred artifacts associated with the battle. Of these, twenty-one have been identified as being directly related to the munitions used by the artillery of both sides. This collection consists of three groups of items; three iron canister plates, seven cuprous canister shot, as well as ten small trapezoidal shaped pieces of lead referred to as "ingots", and one mass of lead ingots fused together. These artifacts and analysis of their locations, combined with historical research have answered some questions regarding the artillery at the Battle of San Jacinto. The analysis and research have also indicated differences in the way in which the two sides deployed their artillery, implying that these differences in the use of projective force influenced the outcome of this battle. This presentation will discuss these artifacts and the results of the analysis (which can also be found in a chapter of the upcoming Texas A&M Press book The Archaeology of Engagement; Conflict and Revolution in the United States").

The Archaeology of Archaeology (Paper, General Session – Museums and Collections, 5:00pm Friday, Paluxy)

Maggie McClain (Atkins)

We've all had to deal with them at some point: collections from projects long past, forgotten once the report was written and the project cleared to proceed. Curation went on the back burner behind new projects with pressing deadlines, until suddenly you receive that permit expiration notice in the mail. Or perhaps you are a grad student assigned to write up an old field school, analyzing artifacts left abandoned in a closet for decades. Such collections present challenges due to missing paperwork, poor organization, and simple human error. These projects may require significant time, energy, and patience to sort through what is present and to prepare the collection for curation. Often, figuring out what occurred on a project may itself require an excavation: digging through cabinets, closets, and boxes to locate artifacts; sifting through piles of paperwork and digital files in search of field documentation to provide context; and carefully analyzing the artifacts and documentation together to reconstruct the past (project). However, there are strategies to streamline this process, and ways to avoid creating such problems for future generations. Furthermore, such "legacy" collections often provide a wealth of information, comparative collections, and unique opportunities for research and publications.

Eagle Cave South Trench 2015: Profile Section 12 (Poster, Eagle Nest Canyon Session, Saturday 11:00am-3:00pm, Texas Ballroom Foyer)

Emily McCuistion (Denali National Park & Preserve)

Profile Section 12 (PS012) is part of the expansive, recently re-exposed south trench wall of Eagle Cave. It lies at a point of transition from superior preservation (just behind the shelter's drip-line) to increasingly fragmented organics and compacted sediments near the back of the shelter. Evaluated in the context of the entire south trench profile, PS012 will aid in understanding site formation and preservation processes. Stand-alone, this preliminary investigation of PS012 highlights changing use over time, represented by latrine deposits, earth oven refuse, fiber artifacts, stone tools, modified wood artifacts, and painted pebbles.

Rapid High Precision Elevation Mapping and Erosion Modeling of a Caddo Mound Site in Henderson County, Texas (Paper, 3D Data in Archaeology Symposium, 4:20pm Friday, Woodbine)

Arlo McKee (Consulting Geoarchaeologist and University of Texas at Dallas)

Lightweight unmanned aerial vehicles (UAVs) have proven to be useful tools to rapidly collect photogrammetric data for mapping archaeological sites and for documenting landscape change. These surveys require considerations of camera specifics, resolution, flight altitude, and speed requirements that can be cumbersome during initial planning stages. This paper will demonstrate how a UAV was used to produce an elevation dataset accurate to the nearest centimeter of the M.S. Roberts Caddo Mound Site (41HE8) with minimal field time. Survey planning was facilitated through the development of an ArcGIS add-in toolbar that accepts user inputs to automatically generate survey waypoints and partition these into a format usable by the UAV autopilot system. This toolbar allows the surveyor to efficiently adapt to in-field study area boundary changes while maintaining optimal field parameters. In addition to providing context for the archaeological investigations at the site, this dataset was used as an input to an erosion model that is helping to address questions concerning mound preservation. This analysis has shown that the mound has lost over 50% of its height and has elongated over the past 85 years.

Archaeological Investigations on the West Side of Plaza de Armas, San Antonio, Bexar County, Texas (Paper, General Session – Archaeology of the Historic Period in Texas, 11:20am Saturday, Paluxy)

Clinton M. M. McKenzie (UTSA Center for Archaeological Research)

Investigations by UTSACAR in 2013-2014 identified remaining intact Spanish Colonial sheet midden deposits and trash pits along the eastern slope of San Pedro Creek in downtown San Antonio. The site forms the west side of Plaza de Armas (Military Plaza). Artifacts and features from these deposits are associated with the use of the site during the Presidio de Bexar period (1722 to circa 1800) as well as residential use from circa 1800 to 1870. Despite being deeply truncated by the creation of the historic Fest-Steves complex circa 1875 to 1880, significant deposits remain in place. The paper presents the history of the site, site formation and deformation, and discusses various features and artifacts.

Digging up (and Passing on) Texas History – One Trowel Full at a Time: The Houston Archeological Society's Educational and Public Outreach Programs (Paper, Texas Archeological Stewards Network Symposium, 3:20pm Friday, Paluxy)

Sharon Menegaz (Education Chairman, Houston Archeology Society) and Linda C. Gorski (Texas Archeological Stewardship Network and President, Houston Archeology Society)
Education has always been a primary goal of the Houston Archeological Society. In 2015, HAS, in consultation with longtime TAS member and Texas history teacher, Sharon Menegaz, fine-tuned its educational and outreach programs. Sharon helped the Society develop new educational materials and hands-on activities that we used with great success in our public outreach and educational presentations across the Houston area. These educational programs ranged from providing fieldwork, lab and classroom activities to groups as diverse as the annual Statewide Health Sciences Summer Institute for teachers K-12 to classroom programs for local schools including Awty International School where kids from around the world learned about Texas archeology. We also presented programs on archeology to historical societies such as the DAR, SRT, DRT, the San Jacinto Battleground Conservancy, the Houston Museum of Natural Science, and the Heritage Society, and environmental groups such as the Texas Master Naturalists, and the Memorial Park Conservancy to promote awareness of archeology in Houston and southeast Texas. In this talk we will demonstrate how these educational and public outreach programs have contributed to a heightened awareness of historical and archeological preservation in the Houston area … and correspondingly to a surge in HAS memberships.

The Archaic Period of Trans-Pecos Texas and Southern New Mexico: New Insights and New Revelations (Paper, General Session – Perspectives on the Paleoindian and Archaic Periods in Texas, 8:40am Saturday, Woodbine)

Myles R. Miller (Versar-GMI) and Tim Graves (Versar-GMI)

Archaeological investigations of the past two decades on Fort Bliss Military Reservation and elsewhere across the Jornada region of Trans-Pecos Texas and southern New Mexico have produced an impressive amount of information on Archaic Period sites and material culture. A contextual and landscape analysis of 3,295 radiocarbon dates from Archaic and early Formative period contexts, including radiocarbon dated settlements, features, technologies, perishable items, and projectile points, has resulted in a new synthesis of Archaic Period adaptations and social evolution. Distinctive subsistence, technological, and social developments can be isolated for much of the Middle and Late Archaic intervals, and the Jornada Archaic can now be securely placed within the broader Archaic traditions of the American Southwest. The high-resolution chronology reveals several trends and transitions - some previously unknown - that relate to topics of archaeological and anthropological significance, including culture-climate interactions, the introduction and spread of maize, and relationships between horticulture and earth oven plant baking. Each of these are related to increasing social complexity and how the structuring and mediation of ecological relationships via social production contributed to the formation of the archaeological record in the form of spiritual sites, communal features, and other material expressions of belief.

Ground Penetrating Radar Data from an Antelope Creek Site (41PT283) (Paper, General Session –Geospatial Mapping and Remote Sensing, 2:40pm Friday, Woodbine)

Michael Mudd (Texas State University) and Robert Z. Selden Jr. (Stephen F. Austin State University)

In June of 2015, a ground penetrating radar (GPR) survey was conducted at an Antelope Creek site (41PT283) located on the Cross Bar Ranch in Potter County, Texas. The raw data were collected using a SIR3000 with a 400MHz antenna along the X-axis of a 13m (X axis) x 14m (Y axis) grid at 50cm intervals. The GPR survey grid was linked to an existing grid mapped during previous investigations at 41PT283 by Texas State University in 2007 and 2008. The archaeological records, artifacts and other materials from these excavations are curated at the Center for Archaeological Studies at Texas State and undergoing analysis for my Master's thesis, which focuses on determining site function and human behavior at 41PT283. With this in mind, the purpose of the GPR survey is to identify potential buried architectural and/or archaeological features that can be further assessed using hand-excavated 1m-x-1m test units. This presentation shall provide an overview of the methodology applied during the GPR survey and preliminary interpretations of the resulting raw data.

Sawing Logs Once More: The Removal and Restoration of a late 1880s Sawmill on the Zapalac Ranch (41FY430) (Paper, General Session – Archaeology of the Historic Period in Texas, 10:40am Saturday, Paluxy)

Stephanie Mueller (Witte Museum)

From the 1880s to at least 1900, the Zapalac Ranch (41FY430) was one of the large local producers of corn, cotton, sugar cane, lumber, and cattle in Fayette and Colorado Counties. By 1884, the ranch had its own railroad spur or switch to transport goods to nearby towns and beyond. Lumber production on the ranch was primarily based out of a two-story building that housed a DeLoach No. 1 variable friction feed sawmill. The Zapalac Family continued to operate the mill for family and business use until the early 1970s. While the mill itself remained in repairable order, the two-story building housing it was starting to collapse. This paper provides a brief overview of the ranch's known historic and prehistoric components and the story of how the Zapalac sawmill was saved to be able to saw logs once more.

¿Dónde está la frontera? (Where is the Frontier?) (Paper, Trans Rio Bravo/Rio Grande International Research Collaboration Symposium, 2:20pm Saturday, Woodbine)

Victoria L. Muñoz (Shumla Archaeological Research and Education Center)

Shumla Archaeological Research and Education Center is working with Mexican historians, archaeologists and iconographers to design a set of procedures and techniques suitable for the documentation, classification, analysis, and interpretation of rock art on both sides of the border. This multi-year collaborative project is funded by Mexico's National Council of Science and Technology, as well as grants received by Shumla. It engages over 20 individuals from both countries, including accomplished researchers and students. Through this partnership, we hope to bridge the gap not only between Mexico and Texas, but also between comparable data sets from our two countries to better understand the hunter-gatherers of this vast region. It's clear that the Rio Grande did not serve as an impenetrable boundary in prehistory and we are limiting ourselves by formulating hypotheses with only a fraction of the data. Shumla will be providing on-site technical training on rock art documentation both in Mexico and in the Lower Pecos. Our Mexican colleagues will be disseminating project results through a permanent seminar, an annual conference, and specialized publications.

Connections: Rock Art across the River of Two Names (Paper, Trans Rio Bravo/Rio Grande International Research Collaboration Symposium, 2:45pm Saturday, Woodbine)

William Breen Murray (Profesor del Departamento de Ciencias Sociales UDEM)

The river with two names (the Rio Grande/Río Bravo) is a formidable north/south political barrier today but in prehistory it seems to have been a significant east-west connection between the continental interior and the Northeast Mexican corridor of the Sierra Madre Oriental and adjoining Gulf Coastal Plain. This paper will explore connections between Texas rock art sites and that found in the Mexican states of Coahuila and Nuevo León, indicating shared motifs and similarities in site contexts.

N

The Use of 3-D GPR As An Aid in the Rediscovery of Spanish Colonial Acequias in San Antonio, Texas
(Paper, General Session –Geo-spatial Mapping and Remote Sensing, 3:20pm Friday, Woodbine)

Kristi Miller Nichols, RPA (Raba Kistner Environmental, Inc.), Laurie M. Steves (EIT), Richard A. Sample (Raba Kistner Environmental, Inc.), Clint Laffere (Raba Kistner Environmental, Inc.)

Archaeologists at Raba Kistner Environmental, Inc. (RKEI) have been utilizing 3-D ground penetrating radar (GPR) surveys to rediscover the locations and document the construction techniques of irrigation ditches in San Antonio, Texas. Using 3-D GPR, in conjunction with EM-31 surveys, archival research, and archaeological backhoe trenching has allowed us to determine under what geomorphological and burial conditions the GPR yields reliable results. This paper reviews recent RKEI projects involving GPR surveys, highlighting the processes and final results during acequia rediscoveries.

Micromorph Mania: A Microstratigraphic Approach to Evaluating Site Formation Processes at Eagle Cave
(Poster, Eagle Nest Canyon Session, Saturday 11:00am-3:00pm, Texas Ballroom Foyer)

Christina Nielsen (Texas State University), Charles Frederick (Consulting Geoarchaeologist), Ken Lawrence (SWCA Environmental Consultants)

Eagle Cave (41VV167) is a large dry rockshelter with deep stratified deposits spanning the Early Archaic through Late Prehistoric periods. Nielsen's thesis research focuses on deposits in the northern sector of the shelter sampled during 1963 excavations by UT-Austin and again a half century later by Texas State University in 2014. My goal is to use multiple lines of evidence to evaluate the natural and cultural formation processes that resulted in the complexly stratified, culturally rich deposits present in Eagle Cave. Our ongoing analysis involves a robust geoarchaeological sampling strategy that included the collection of micromorphological (micromorph) samples. The 13 relevant micromorph samples captured approximately 24 of the 85 total stratigraphic layers identified in the field. This poster highlights the benefits and difficulties of collecting micromorph samples from fragile rockshelter deposits and shows how the analysis of the resulting slabbed samples and thin sections can aid in evaluating site formation processes.

O

Build It and They Will Come: Examining Burned Rock Feature Construction and Re-use During the Late Archaic at 41CV286 (Paper, General Session – New Methods and Research in Texas Archaeology, 2:00pm Saturday, Permian)

Eric R. Oksanen (Texas Department of Transportation)

TxDOT considers the places on the landscape that people liked to settle, what traces their activities might have left, and in one case in Coryell County (41CV286), how repeat visits over centuries reveals a complex history of site-use. During 2008 testing and 2009 data recovery excavations, TxDOT sampled burned-rock features and recovered a variety of lithic dart points, tools, debitage and faunal remains before efforts were abandoned due to extreme rainfall. The initial suite of AMS dates on charcoal and bone indicate occupations from the Late Archaic through the Late Prehistoric, and varying intensity of occupation, feature construction and re-use. Research at the adjacent Fort Hood examined the relationship between burned rock features and middens and the landscape. At 41CV286 there is at least one midden, but other features might have developed into middens but for being buried under alluvium. To investigate and characterize the potential variability in the features, and whether they were used briefly for a short period or repeatedly over a long period, additional radiocarbon dates from animal bone is compared with the wood dates. A sample of the lithic assemblage is analyzed for measures of contemporaneity and technical and material change through time.

A New Beginning for the Old Socorro Mission del Sur (Paper, General Session – Archaeology of the Historic Period in Texas, 9:40am Saturday, Paluxy)

Tiffany Osburn (Texas Historical Commission)

The Old Socorro Mission was established in 1684 in Socorro, TX. Previous investigations of the Mission in the 1980s and 90s identified many of the adobe wall alignments composing the mission complex. In early 2015 this significant site became part of Texas state public lands. The site is designated a State Antiquities Landmark and was acquired by the Texas Historical Commission through a cooperative mitigation agreement with the Texas Department of Transportation. Initiatives being developed for the site include ongoing investigations to reestablish the location of previous excavations, prospect for the campo santo, and identify the location of the Piro village associated with the mission. Recent work suggests the presence of mission period occupations north of the mission within the recently acquired tract.

P

Eagle Cave South Trench 2015: Initial Observations from PS015 (Poster, Eagle Nest Canyon Session, Saturday 11:00am-3:00pm, Texas Ballroom Foyer)

Victoria C. Pagano (Texas State University)

The 2015 field season in Eagle Cave revealed interesting stratigraphy and preservation in the south trench profile. This poster presents the preliminary findings from PS015, a fiber-rich profile section located on the east side of the trench close to the dripline. The profile has unique preservation of mixed fiber and other organic remains, a stark contrast to the later deposition events found in the western profiles further towards the back wall of Eagle Cave. Within this fiber zone are dense concentrations of fire cracked rock. Interestingly, PS015 revealed numerous coprolites, several nearly complete lechuguilla central stems, and other perishable artifacts -- such as faunal remains and fiber artifacts, but very little chipped or ground stone tools. PS015 may represent a different suite of activities than what is preserved at other sections of the trench. Various samples -- C14, geomorph, soil -- were collected as the profile was described and photographed for 3D-modeling.

Can Flake Size Provide Meaningful Information about Flint Knapping Events? (Poster, Saturday 8:30am-10:30am, Texas Ballroom Foyer)

Scott Pletka (Texas Department of Transportation)

The most frequently discovered evidence of past human activity is stone tools and the debris left from the production of those stone tools. The stone tools can tell a story about what activities took place. But what can we expect to learn from the stone tool manufacturing debris (called flakes) that we often find? Experimental studies suggest that the distribution of flake sizes produced by flint knapping takes a predictable form, and the distribution varies in predicable ways during flint knapping. For example, the range of flake sizes generally decreases during flint knapping, because the core being struck is getting smaller. We might be able to use such observations to accurately interpret archeological collections, if the relationships can be modeled statistically. This poster builds on previous work by presenting a new statistical model that might better capture the range of flint knapping stages represented in a collection of flakes.

Geoarchaeology and Rockshelter Evolution along McCutchen Branch (Paper, Barnhill Rockshelter Symposium, 8:20am Saturday, Permian)

Shane J. Prochnow (Chevron) and Carol Ann Macaulay-Jameson (Baylor University)

McCutchen Creek has played a pivotal role in the formation and preservation of numerous rockshelters and other archaeological features on the Barnhill Ranch in Coryell County, Texas. The drainage system has carved a progression of bedrock overhangs at the Commanche Peak-Edwards Formation contract that contain older fill in downstream exposures and progressively younger aged fill in upstream exposures. Active overhang cutting occurs near the knick point of tributaries. The alluvial fill within these rockshelters is loosely correlated to terrace sediment packages that were dated using both radiocarbon and artifact styles. The alluvial terrace sediments were fit into a chronostratigraphic framework separated by paleosols (stable buried surfaces) similar to that previously developed for Fort Hood (Nordt, 1992). The alluvial stratigraphy coupled with the conceptual model of rockshelter formation for the McCutchen Creek drainage explains differential preservation of archaeological material amongst the several rockshelters at the Barnhill Ranch, and enables the prediction of buried cultural material in several different geomorphic settings.

R

Las Camas or Cupboards? An Analysis of Supposed Sleeping Features from Hinds Cave (41VV456) in Val Verde County, Texas (Paper, General Session – New Methods and Research in Texas Archaeology, 4:00pm Saturday, Permian)

Casey Wayne Riggs (Texas A&M University)

Since 1975 a variety of features from Hinds Cave (41VV456) in the Lower Pecos have been presented as sleeping activity related site furniture. In 2014 an analysis of four of these features indicates a much different use by Archaic hunter-gatherer inhabitants of the site. Rather than use as beds, this analysis suggests said features are related to storage for both botanical foods (primarily wild onion [Allium spp.]) and plant fiber, specifically from agaves (Agavoideae) and grass (Poaceae), in various stages of retting. This project brings the original use of these features more in line with recent findings of plant-lined storage pits throughout western North America. Additionally this analysis posits a unique caching behavior of storing prepared fiber within the Lower Pecos archaeological region of Texas.

A Consideration of Labor Expenditure in Archaic Biface Production in the Rio Grande Plains (Paper, General Session – New Methods and Research in Texas Archaeology, 2:40pm Saturday, Permian)

Christopher W. Ringstaff (Texas Department of Transportation)

Ongoing excavations by TxDOT at site 41ZP191 and other sites in the Rio Grande Plains have uncovered Middle to Late Archaic lithic production features which have presented interpretive challenges. This study uses an experimental archeological approach to address one line of inquiry: labor expenditure. A total of 35 biface reduction experiments was conducted to quantify the time required to reduce quarried blanks into finished thin bifaces. The goal of these experiments is to produce comparative data for a quantitative interpretation of known biface production features which vary in size and, hypothetically, labor expenditure. Using siliceous gravels from South Texas for the experiments, total production time was recorded for each blank reduced. In addition, blank, failed tool, and finished tool attributes were measured and debitage collected and quantified from each experiment. The descriptive statistics generated from these experiments provide a basis for interpreting labor expenditure inputs in selected biface production features from the region. Variability in labor expenditure is considered in differentiating biface maintenance/ replacement from mass production gearing-up events. The results of this comparative study are integrated with prior minimum analytic nodule and technological analyses to provide a framework for making inferences on technological organization, mobility, and raw material economy.

TARL Today (Paper, TARL Today Symposium, 2:50pm Saturday, Paluxy)

Brian E. Roberts (Texas Archeological Research Lab)

TARL has seen significant changes in leadership and institutional support over the past few years. Brian Roberts, the Director of TARL, has been on the job for a little over a year and will share his thoughts on UT's institutional commitment to TARL, both in general and with respect to a number of new initiatives.

How to Capture a Photograph worth a Thousand words: Photographic Documentation of Rock Art in the Lower Pecos Canyonlands of Texas (Paper, General Session – New Methods in Rock Art Research, 10:40am Saturday, Woodbine)

Jerod L. Roberts (Shumla Archaeological Research and Education Cente), Victoria L. Muñoz (Shumla Archaeological Research and Education Center), and Carolyn E. Boyd (Shumla Archaeological Research and Education Center)

Digital photography provides increasingly sophisticated applications that are invaluable to rock art researchers. Shumla Archaeological Research and Education Center relies heavily on many of these applications to document, preserve, and analyze rock art—such as 3D modeling through Structure from Motion (SfM) photogrammetry, multi-focal stacking, color management, and digital field microscopy for stratigraphic analyses. Depending on which applications are used, there are important considerations that should be addressed to ensure the collection and management of accurate visual data. This presentation will discuss some of these applications and how they are being implemented in the extensive photographic documentation of one of the most complex and threatened rock art sites in North America—the pictographic mural of Rattlesnake Canyon.

The Early Archaic and Paleoindian Occupation of Kelley Cave (41VV164) (Paper, General Session – Perspectives on the Paleoindian and Archaic Periods in Texas, 9:20am Saturday, Woodbine)

Daniel Rodriguez

Excavations undertaken in 2013-2014 have uncovered deep cultural features in Kelley Cave (41VV164). Recent radiocarbon assays date the lowest features at the site to the Early Archaic and Late Paleoindian time periods. Numerous radiocarbon dates, and signals of faunal activity suggest the shelter was intensely occupied during the latter part of the Early Archaic. Features dating to the Early Archaic show the presence of earth ovens and a stone-lined cyst in the shelter ca. 7500 cal B.P. Immediately below these features, a stone slab griddle was uncovered and recently radiocarbon dated to 11,700-11,300 cal B.P. making it broadly contemporaneous with the events of Bone Bed 2 in Bonfire Shelter (41VV218).

S

Fuentes archivísticas para la etnohistoria del noreste de Mexico y de Texas (Archival Resources for Ethnohistorical Studies of Northeastern Mexico and Texas) (Paper, Trans Rio Bravo/Rio Grande International Research Collaboration Symposium, 3:35pm Saturday, Woodbine)

Martín Salinas Rivera (Archivo Municipal de Reynosa/Archivo Histórico de Reynosa)

The ethnohistorical knowledge of the Native American populations in the geographic area that now includes the states of Tamaulipas, Nuevo Leon, Coahuila and Texas comes from disseminated archives in the Americas and Europe. Part of their existence lingers from episodes of exploration and colonization of this vast territory that was slowly occupied by the European and novohispanic sociopolitical structure, since the first half of the sixteenth century. Knowledge of the Native Americans in the Coastal Plain and neighboring areas was sporadically recorded. The archival resources are essential to rebuild their historical presence, adaptations, and cultural changes during colonization and their social decline. This work presents the available archival resources that might be of interest of communities as well as academics from a variety of disciplines such as cultural anthropology, history, Native American studies, archaeology, ecology, linguistics, and other related disciplines.

Using Photogrammetry to Document, Analyze and Reverse-Engineer Grave Markers (Paper, 3D Data in Archaeology Symposium, 4:40pm Friday, Woodbine)

Robert Z. Selden Jr. (Stephen F. Austin State University)

There are a wide range of applications for three-dimensional (3D) data in archaeology, and a diverse array of methods for collecting and analyzing those data. In this presentation, free 3D photogrammetry software (Autodesk 123D Catch) is used to document a series of grave markers. The data are subsequently exported to Geomagic Design X to demonstrate and briefly discuss the various potential analyses that might be used to illustrate the effects of preservation treatments and marker degradation through time. Further, one marker is reverse-engineered, illustrating the capacity of 3D modeling to expedite the process of design, should elements warrant replacement. Additional benefits of documenting the markers in 3D includes public outreach and public interaction through social media. Autodesk's 123D Catch allows users to render videos of each model and export them to YouTube, where they can be shared with a global audience. The capacity of these tools to expand the scope of our efforts to document and analyze grave markers is substantial.

The Index of Texas Archaeology: Open Access Gray Literature from the Lone Star State (Poster, Saturday 8:30am-10:30am, Texas Ballroom Foyer)

Robert Z. Selden Jr. (Stephen F. Austin State University), C. Britt Bousman (Texas State University)

Since 2008, cultural resource management (CRM) projects carried out under the auspices of a Texas Antiquities Code permit have been required to submit, as one part of the reporting requirements, a redacted report. The goal of the Index of Texas Archaeology (ITA) is to make those reports digitally accessible in a format that is simple to navigate, search engine optimized, and indexed by multiple search engines. In its current form, all reports would be indexed by Google within seven days of posting, and citations can be tracked using Google Scholar. While authors would be provided a monthly readership report, the agencies/firms can customize reports to see when and where their reports have been downloaded. Additionally, users can opt into various RSS feeds where they will be provided an email when a report of interest is uploaded by using keywords (i.e., Toyah, Antelope Creek, Lithics, Ceramics, etc.). Using the Berkeley Electronic Press (bepress) platform and Creative Commons licensing, the ITA would provide a highly searchable and open access outlet for redacted reports from across the State of Texas, making these reports and data available to scholars and students of the North American archaeology for the first time.

The New Witte Museum and Archaeology (Paper, General Session – Museums and Collections, 4:40pm Friday, Paluxy)

Harry J. Shafer (Witte Museum)

The Witte Museum in San Antonio is undergoing a major transformation. The expanded campus will include the new 10,000 square foot Mays Gallery and Events Center and the completely renovated main building will feature new permanent exhibits in Texas Deep Time featuring the Cretaceous Period in the Valero Great Hall and Dinosaur Gallery, new and updated McCLean Family Texas Wild illustrating the landscapes of Texas, and the People of the Pecos featuring a series of exhibits with life-size mannequins to show the hunter-gatherer Archaic cultural lifeway and rock art. Each of these major exhibits also will have lab areas for teaching and interactive programs. The Mays Family Gallery and Events Center will open on May of 2016 and feature Maya: Hidden World Revealed, the most comprehensive exhibit of the Maya ever presented. The Texas Deep Time will open in the late fall of 2017.

Early Norwegian Settlers on the Texas Frontier: Uncovering the Home of Cleng Peerson (Paper, Texas Archeological Stewards Network Symposium, 2:20pm Friday, Paluxy)

Rebecca Shelton (Texas Historical Commission), and Bryan Jameson (Texas Archeological Stewards Network)

The search for the home of Cleng Peerson, founding father of Texas's earliest Norwegian settlement in Bosque County, began when a curious landowner contacted the Texas Historical Commission (THC) History Division. The THC enlisted the assistance of Texas Archeological Stewards Network members Bryan Jameson and Art Tawater. After extensive archival research and field investigations, TASN members verified that Peerson acquired 320 acres outside of Clifton in 1859, had given 160 acres to Ovee Colwick in 1860 in exchange for a place to live and be cared for in his final years, and the landowner was indeed living on property that contained the remains of the homestead. Excavations revealed the remains of a stone house with an earthen walled cellar. The floorplan aligns with the 1896 insurance documents of the Colwick home. Numerous family histories share the story of Peerson's commitment to the community and provide pictorial evidence of the various construction phases of the house through multiple generations of the Colwick family. In 2015, the homestead was nominated to the National

Register of Historic Places because of its potential to yield important information regarding the acculturation of a relatively isolated immigrant community which is underrepresented in the archeological record.

Raman Spectroscopy of FCR from Texas Earth Ovens (Paper, General Session – New Methods and Research in Texas Archaeology, 4:40pm Saturday, Permian)

Laura Short (Texas A&M University)

Macrobotanicals, usually in the form of identifiable charcoal, have formed the basis of our archaeological evidence of what was cooked in earth ovens, and microbotanicals such as phytoliths, pollen, and starch grains are expanding that knowledge. There are, however, still limitations: for example, inulin does not have a microbotanical proxy. Inulin is the primary carbohydrate for many important plant foods such as onion, camas, agave and sotol. Researchers use vibrational spectroscopy to characterizes a substance by measuring the change in a light's wavelength as it passes through the substance. Raman spectroscopy is a type of vibrational spectroscopy that has been used extensively in art and archaeology but not yet applied to fire cracked rock. This presentation reports on the initial results of a Raman spectroscopy analysis of organic residues on fire cracked rock from earth ovens on Fort Hood, attempting to develop a new technique for direct evidence of what was processed in earth ovens.

Identifying the Archaeological Potential of the Rio Grande Valley Civil War Trail (Paper, General Session – Archaeology of the Historic Period in Texas, 11:40am Saturday, Paluxy)

Russell K. Skowronek (University of Texas Rio Grande Valley)

The "Rio Grande Valley Civil War Trail" (www.utrgv.edu/civilwar-trail) was launched in February of 2015. Developed by the Community Historical Archaeology Project with Schools (CHAPS) Program of the University of Texas Rio Grande Valley with federal, state and local partners it is the only trail in Texas dedicated to the era of the American Civil War. Connecting Laredo and Brownsville the trail follows 200 miles of the Rio Grande's journey to the Gulf of Mexico. Along the rail are battlefields, forts, and historic buildings and long vanished town sites, a salt-mine, and sites associated with the south-bound "underground railroad." Little archeological work has been conducted at these sites. This presentation explores the potential for archaeological research along the trail.

Unique findings within an analysis of a single coprolite from Conejo Shelter, Texas (Poster, Saturday 8:30am-10:30am, Texas Ballroom Foyer)

Elanor Sonderman (Texas A&M University), Crystal Dozier (Texas A&M University), Morgan Smith (Texas A&M University)

This study examines the floral and faunal remains from a single coprolite from Conejo Shelter just north of the confluence of the Rio Grande and the Pecos River, in Val Verde county, TX. Floral macrobotanical analysis revealed a high density of lechuguilla and sotol fibers. Calcium oxalate crystals confirm the ingestion of Opuntia. Palynological analysis found evidence for a variety of plants with known economic and medicinal uses, with pollen from the Liliaceae (new: Asparagales) family predominating. Zooarchaeological analysis found the remains of a small rodent, evidently eaten whole, with no indication of preparation or cooking. Notably, the bones, scales, and fang of a snake in the Viperidae family were also recovered from the coprolite, which is the first direct archaeological evidence of venomous snake consumption known to the researchers. With the exception of the Viperidae remains, this coprolite evidence is consistent with previous research at Conejo Shelter (Alexander 1974, Bryant 1974). While the stratigraphy at Conejo shelter is fairly well established, Lens 9, where this coprolite was excavated, has not been directly dated. Future radiocarbon dating of the coprolite remains may elucidate a better understanding of this unique gastrological event in association with the paleoenvironment of south Texas approximately 2,000 years ago.

Two Independent Methods for Dating Rock Art: Age Determination of Paint and Oxalate Layers at Eagle Cave, TX (Poster, Eagle Nest Canyon Session, Saturday 11:00am-3:00pm, Texas Ballroom Foyer)

Karen L. Steelman (University of Central Arkansas), Carolyn E. Boyd (Shumla Archaeological Research & Education Center)

Using two independent methods, we provide reliable age estimates for three Pecos River Style figures at Eagle Cave in Langtry, TX. To obtain direct dates for the paintings, we employed plasma oxidation of the organic binders in the paint layer followed by accelerator mass spectrometry. For minimum and maximum ages, we acid treated the overlying and underneath accretion layers to isolate calcium oxalate for combustion and 14C measurement. The radiocarbon dates for the three paint samples are statistically indistinguishable, with a weighted average of 3280±70 years BP calibrated to 1740-1420 cal BC at 2 sigma (95.4% probability). Overlying accretion layers are younger and underlying accretion layers are older. This correctly ordered, chronological stratigraphy of the accretion and paint layers supports the validity of both dating methods. As new high-resolution excavations are underway at Eagle Cave, the rock paintings can now be studied alongside excavated cultural deposits to provide a more complete understanding of this hunter-gather society.

Cultural Resource Subsurface Survey and Archeological Monitoring of the Nau Center for Texas Cultural Heritage, Houston, Harris County, Texas (Paper, General Session – Archaeology of the Houston Area, 8:20am Saturday, Paluxy)

Eleanor Stoddart (Moore Archeological Consulting, Inc.)

In early 2015, Moore Archeological Consulting, Inc., conducted both cultural resource subsurface survey field investigations and archeological construction monitoring of the proposed Nau Center for Texas Cultural Heritage. The focus of the investigations was on Blocks 119 and 161, in downtown Houston, Harris County, Texas. At the time of the mechanical scraping program, the study area had been partially disturbed by years of urban development and demolition. The archeological excavation uncovered remnants of one of Houston's earliest residential neighborhoods dating from the middle of the nineteenth century. Although covered by asphalt and dirt parking lots, 12 features (including cisterns, brick pavements and trash pits) were exposed during selected blading of Block 161 as Block 119 was found to have been previously excavated during an earlier archeological investigation. Over 2100 artifacts, including glass, ceramics, architectural and personal items, as well as faunal remains were recovered from Block 161. These artifacts and features shed light on some of the moderately wealthy, early inhabitants of Houston during a time where Houston was undergoing rapid economic and cultural development. In this paper, the results of this investigation are compared to other urban sites, both wealthy and poor, in Houston during the same time period.

Kemosabe: A New Multi-Component Prehistoric Site Complex Adjacent To the Guadalupe River, Kerr County, Texas (Paper, Texas Archeological Stewards Network Symposium, 2:40pm Friday, Paluxy)

Steve Stoutamire (Texas Archeological Stewardship Network)

The Kemosabe site complex encompasses over 80 acres of private land adjacent to the Guadalupe River. To date, this complex has yielded projectile points that date from Lower, Early Archaic to Toyah Phase, Late Prehistoric. Four middens, three fire-cracked rock scatters and two lithic scatter/workshops have been recorded on the property. Surface traverses, auger hole testing, back hoe trenching, unit excavation, stratigraphic and sedimentary analysis and an aerial drone survey employing photogammetry have been conducted. The Kemosabe complex appears similar to the Gatlin Site (41KR621), which was discovered as TxDOT was constructing Spur 98 across the Guadalupe River. The two sites are comparable in topographic and geographic setting relative to the river. Investigations at Gatlin were lauded for its contributions to the archeological record as well as being one of the largest excavations of Early Archaic deposits in Central Texas. Gatlin excavations also yielded an unusually high recovery of Early and Middle Archaic dart points. The Kemosabe complex has already yielded cultural material in context from Early Archaic and younger sediments. Excavations and analysis of material at the site are planned since there are no time constraints on investigations, thus allowing for a thorough study of this promising prehistoric complex.

T

WPA Archaeology: Revisiting the Harrell Site Collections (Paper, TARL Today Symposium, 1:50pm Saturday, Paluxy)

Marybeth S.F. Tomka (Texas Archeological Research Lab) and Lauren H. Bussiere (Texas Archeological Research Lab)

In this paper we will present the ongoing rehabilitation of the WPA collections from the Harrell Site (41YN1). We will examine the pitfalls of old collection management techniques and the wonders of 21stcentrury technology to make collections accessible.

Utilizing Archival Information to Re-Locate or "Stumble Upon" Lost Archeological Sites (Poster, Saturday 8:30am-10:30am, Texas Ballroom Foyer)

Waldo Troell (Texas Department of Transportation)

For a multitude of reasons, many of the archeology sites recorded in the first half of the 20th century are plotted incorrectly or not at all on the Texas Archeological Sites Atlas. Several Texas Department of Transportation projects in Northeast Texas have resulted in the relocation of previously lost sites, which have emerged still relatively intact. Traditional archival tools, such as historic highway maps, photos, and TARL site files not currently on the Atlas, can help identify the location of these lost sites. This poster will examine some of the relocated sites and the archival tools that were used to find them. Sites rediscovered include Caddo farmsteads, villages, and two mounds originally identified during The University of Texas 1930's excavations and the River Basin Survey from the 1940's.

Use-Wear Analysis of Utilized Flakes from Barnhill Rockshelter #3 (41CV1646) (Paper, Barnhill Rockshelter Symposium, 9:40am Saturday, Permian)

Kendall Turner (Baylor University)

Utilized flakes were a common artifact type recovered during excavations at Barnhill Rockshelter #3 (41CV1646) during the 2015 Baylor University Archaeological Field School. This study sought to understand how a sampling of these utilized-flake tools were used based on microscopic use-wear analysis. In order to identify the characteristic signatures of different types of use wear, an experiment was carried out using flake tools made from the same chert source as that of the prehistoric flake tools. The experiment identified characteristics of use wear from scraping hide and wood; and cutting grass, hide, bone, and meat. Seven utilized-flake tools were randomly selected for analysis and they were examined under both stereoscopic and compound light microscopes. Similar types of use wear were identified on several of the utilized-flake tools. This presentation will conclude by addressing the challenges of use-wear analysis.

V

Al otro lado del Río Grande: los escasos estudios binacionales en Nuevo León, México (On the other side of the Rio Grande: the few binational studies of Nuevo Leon, Mexico) (Paper, Trans Rio Bravo/Rio Grande International Research Collaboration Symposium, 1:55pm Saturday, Woodbine)

Moises Valadez Moreno (Profesor Investigador del Instituto Nacional de Antropología e Historia en Nuevo León - INAH Nuevo León)

A diferencia de otras áreas como Chihuahua, Sonora o Baja California, la región noreste de México se ha caracterizado por la escasez y poco interés de investigadores estadounidenses para el desarrollo de estudios arqueológicos. Dicha situación la explicamos por la falta de comunicación y convenios binacionales que faciliten la participación de colegas texanos en proyectos del INAH, así como el acceso de los arqueólogos mexicanos a proyectos que se desarrollan en Texas. A lo largo de la ponencia haremos un recuento de los trabajos de prospección arqueológica de superficie y excavación que hemos llevado los últimos 25 años en Nuevo León, mostrando el tipo de sitios y restos materiales característicos de esta región y al final hablaremos de los posibles convenios y proyectos binacionales que podríamos realizar a ambos lados del Río Bravo. Unlike other areas such as Chihuahua, Sonora or Baja California, the northeastern region of Mexico has been characterized by the scarcity and little interest from U.S. researchers for the development of archaeological studies. This situation explained it by the lack of communication and binational agreements that facilitate the participation of fellow Texans in the INAH projects, as well as the access of Mexican archaeologists to projects being developed in Texas. Throughout the paper we will do a recount of the works of archaeological survey of surface and excavation that we have taken 25 years in Nuevo Leon, showing the type of sites and material remains characteristic of this region and in the end talk of possible agreements and binational projects that we could perform on both sides of the Rio Grande.

Andean Burial Rites: An Anthropological Study of Human Immolation within Pre-Columbian Inca Society (Poster, Saturday 8:30am-10:30am, Texas Ballroom Foyer)

Ashley Vance (St. Edward's University) and Molly Minus (St. Edward's University, McNair Research Director)

Human immolation within Inca society manifested in a variety of forms, including the ritual of Qhapaq Hucha, as well as runa, warrior, and Necropampa sacrifices. This research examines the underlying political and religious motivations behind this specialized ritual, paying special attention to Aqllas, and the profile of selected sacrificial victims. This study utilized various 16th century Spanish accounts as well as archaeological reports to illustrate the motivations and consequences of Inca human immolation. Human sacrifice provided the Inca with a medium of communication with their deities and helped to synthesize the vast Inca Empire. Qhapaq Hucha was a ritual designed to integrate subjugated communities as well as continuously establishing the authority of the Inca over distant regions.

It's not an Illustration; it's a Graphic Database: Rock Art Documentation in the Digital Age (Paper, General Session – New Methods in Rock Art Research, 11:20am Saturday, Woodbine)

Lindsay A. Vermillion (Shumla Archaeological Research and Education Center and Texas State University), Carolyn E. Boyd (Shumla Archaeological Research and Education Center and Texas State University)

Shumla incorporates new technologies that are revolutionizing rock art illustration and documentation. This presentation discusses the method developed by Shumla to engage these technologies in the production of graphic databases. Using Adobe Photoshop and a Wacom Cintiq Interactive Pen Display, digital Photoshop layers are used to graphically document data for individual figures. These living documents include accurate scale illustrations and the color calibrated and enhanced photographs used to produce the illustrations. Additional layers serve as maps documenting locations of analyses conducted in the field, such as digital microscopy to determine paint stratigraphy, non-destructive elemental analyses of the pigment, and collected sample locations for radiocarbon dating. This approach not only increases data integrity and replicability, it also provides a dynamic, visual record for individual rock art figures and, collectively, entire rock art murals.

Long-Term Phosphate Experiment (Poster, Saturday 8:30am-10:30am, Texas Ballroom Foyer)

Lindsay A. Vermillion (Texas State University), Ken Lawrence, (SWCA), and Texas State Experimental Archaeology Club (Texas State University)

In the fall of 2013, the Experimental Archaeology Club at Texas State was contacted by Ken Lawrence, an archaeologist working in Austin, TX, to aid in a long-term experiment. He was looking to measure the phosphates sampled from a potential archaeological site to determine the likelihood that cultural activities occurred there without digging a giant hole. Through his research on phosphate analysis (which is considered a widely used and accepted method), he concluded that experiments have been conducted to determine the validity of phosphate sampling, but none have ever taken an initial sampling of the natural phosphate levels before the cultural activity has taken place within an area, and then compare it to the levels after the activity occurred. Throughout the course of the next few years, the Experimental Club will perform numerous archaeological experiments replicating ancient cultural activities (earth ovens, pottery making and firing, plant processing, animal processing, flint-knapping, etc...). These activities should change the levels of phosphate found within the soil of the study area. Periodically, more samples will be taken for comparative analysis.

An Overview of the 2015 Baylor University Archaeological Field School at Barnhill Rockshelter #3 (41CV1646), Coryell County, Texas (Paper, Barnhill Rockshelter Symposium, 8:00am Saturday, Permian)

Vincent Villarreal (Baylor University)

This presentation provides an overview of the excavations conducted this summer by nine students who attended the Baylor University Archaeological Field School at Barnhill Rockshelter #3 (41CV1646) in Coryell County, Texas. We focused primarily on the upper deposits and completed a total of 18 units, 48 levels, and found six features dating to the Austin and Toyah Phases of the Late Prehistoric Period. This presentation will describe these features and their associated artifacts and biotic remains within the rockshelter's spatial and temporal context.

W

Disappeared Three Rivers Red-on-Terracotta Bowl (Paper, General Session – Museums and Collections, 5:20pm Friday, Paluxy)

Robin Gay Wakeland

Three Rivers red-on-terracotta ceramics spanned the Permian Basin, El Paso region, Villa Ahumada, Chihuahua, Mexico, north to the Santa Fe River, and west to Swartz Ruin, for 200 years ca. 1100-1250 C.E. H.P. Mera published a grainy photo of a Three Rivers red-on-terracotta bowl in 1931. Besides its typology, the only information he gave was "Alves Collection", and Doña Ana Missile Range (Fort Bliss) as its location. Unfortunately, this bowl is currently disappeared, without any further trace in the public record. Public records requests to the Museum of New Mexico, University of Texas at El Paso Centennial Museum, Arizona State Museum, Peabody Museum, and Fort Bliss army base failed to locate it. Published reports indicated Elieen Alves and other members of the Texas Archaeological and Paleontological Society excavated at Fort Bliss during this time and collected artifacts, including a Three Rivers red-on-terracotta bowl. Recorded pre-1931 site excavations within the Doña Ana missile range are Coe Lake Pueblo and Rifle Range Pueblo. Adjacent excavations within temporal proximity are Country Club Pueblo, Old Coe Ranch (synonymous with Cox Ranch), and Doña Ana Rifle Range sites. Photos of the disappeared bowl, public records, and maps illustrate this presentation.

Unidentified Ceramics in Southwestern Collections (Poster, Saturday 8:30am-10:30am, Texas Ballroom Foyer)

Robin Gay Wakeland

The Bureau of Land Management Carlsbad district and a private museum have ceramic sherds in their collections which remain unidentified. Although they resemble Jornada Red, San Andres red-on-terracotta, Three Rivers red-on-terracotta, Rio Grande glaze A red, and/or Lincoln black-on-red, they lie undetermined. Color photos illustrate the sherds. Contact information is given for archaeologists who wish to contribute knowledge.

Archaeology at the Fulcher Site (41BS1495): A Multi-component Open Campsite along the Lower Reaches of Terlingua Creek, Brewster County, Texas (Paper, Big Bend Archeology Symposium, 4:10pm Saturday, Paluxy)

Richard W. Walter (Center for Big Bend Studies, Sul Ross State University)

In March 2005 and April 2006, The Center for Big Bend Studies conducted archaeological investigations at the Fulcher site. Based on previous visits to the site, it was known that small, charred corn cobs were eroding out of a nearby midden deposit with a peculiar thermal feature of stone and mortar construction. This coupled with the presence of late arrowpoints and ceramics of the Protohistoric and Historic periods warranted further investigations. Findings from the surface collection and test excavations are discussed.

Archaeological and Geological Test Excavations at Site 41HM61, Hamilton County, Central Texas: Life along the Leon River During Archaic and Late Prehistoric Times (Paper, General Session – New Methods and Research in Texas Archaeology, 3:20pm Saturday, Permian)

Richard A. Weinstein (Coastal Environments, Inc.), Charles D. Frederick (Consulting Geoarchaeologist), Jon C. Lohse (Coastal Environments, Inc.)

From September through November 2011, and again in September 2013, Coastal Environments, Inc., under contract to the Texas Department of Transportation, conducted archaeological and geological test excavations at site 41HM61 to determine if that locale was eligible for the National Register of Historic Places. Aided by personnel from Archeological & Environmental Consultants, LLC, and the Center for Big Bend Studies at Sul Ross State University, plus Dr. Charles D. Frederick, it was determined that the site contained intact, finely stratified cultural deposits, separated both horizontally and vertically, extending from the late Middle Archaic period to the Late Prehistoric and/or Protohistoric periods (ca. 2460 B.C. to A.D. 1600). Such stratification allowed the investigators to offer a relatively concise picture of life among those hunter-gatherer groups that sporadically included the Leon River valley within their range of exploitation. Particularly important were the results of AMS radiocarbon dates from various organic remains. When coupled with diagnostic projectile points and associated burned-rock and mussel-shell features, those dates allowed for a fine-grained interpretation of hunter-gatherer subsistence over the roughly 4,000 years that the site was utilized. It also was possible to identify local environmental changes that would have affected subsistence strategies and living conditions.

Data Collection at 41BX274: Analysis of Remote Sensing Anomalies and the Perez Ranch Jacal (Paper, General Session –Geo-spatial Mapping and Remote Sensing, 3:00pm Friday, Woodbine)

Jonathan Welch (Texas Tech University)

Archaeological investigations were conducted during Spring 2015 by Texas Tech University at the Perez Ranch Site (41BX274), located along the Medina River in the southwestern portion of Bexar County, Texas. The Perez Ranch was owned and operated by Juan Ygnacio Perez, a direct descendant of Spanish settlers and husband to Clemencia Hernandez, the granddaughter of Andres Hernandez, the first private rancher in Texas. The archaeological investigations focused on two areas, Area A and B. Excavations of Area A examined the cause of the GPR and Magnetometer anomalies approximately 2m east of the eastern portion of the stone house foundation excavated by CAR in 2007. Through excavation, it was determined that the GPR and Magnetometer anomalies were caused by a burn event and debris pile from the stone house foundation. Excavations of Area B explored a jacal structure, a folk style architecture constructed via the use of poles placed into the ground, located 25-30m southwest of the stone house foundation. Although analysis of artifacts is currently being conducted, some preliminary conclusions can be drawn about the construction methods, age, and potential methods of restoring and preserving the jacal structure from further damage.

Curing Common Ailments: Medicinal Use of Plants at Barnhill Rockshelter #3 (Paper, Barnhill Rockshelter Symposium, 10:00am Saturday, Permian)

Sarah Welle (Baylor University)

Over fifty plant species have been identified from the carbonized botanical remains recovered from four years of excavations at Barnhill Rockshelter #3 (41CV1646). These plant species were utilized by the Late Prehistoric inhabitants of the rockshelter as firewood, food and medicine. Ethnobotanical accounts describe how Native Americans used individual plant species for medicinal purposes. This presentation will, instead, focus on seven common health problems – gastrointestinal ailments, headaches and body aches, dermatological conditions, bites, cuts, colds and fevers, that the inhabitants of the rockshelter possibly suffered and the plants they might have used to treat them.

The Who, What, Where, When, and Why of Clovis Blade Manufacturing in Texas (Paper, General Session – Perspectives on the Paleoindian and Archaic Periods in Texas, 10:00am Saturday, Woodbine)

Thomas Williams (Texas State University)

Blade manufacturing is a recognized facet of Clovis Technology in Texas and is present in numerous assemblages, including the Gault Site, Pavo Real, and Wilson-Leonard. A number of studies have presented good data on various aspects of blade production and Clovis technology in general. Despite this, questions remain as to the precise nature of Clovis blade technology. Careful excavation and surface finds have revealed the spread of this technology across Texas as well as providing associated ages. These assemblages have also contributed to understanding the reduction sequence used to produce blades. What is less clear is precisely why blades were produced and what purpose they served. Finally, the origin of Clovis blade manufacturing still requires in-depth analysis. This paper will focus on the "who, what, where, when, and why" of Clovis blade production in Texas and highlight what we know and what remains to be addressed.

Everyone Is Doing It: How to Document an Archaeological Site in 3D (Paper, 3D Data in Archaeology Symposium, 5:00pm Friday, Woodbine)

Mark D. Willis (Blanton & Associates)

This presentation is a primer on the latest techniques being used around the world to document our prehistory in 3D. Low cost methods from cell phone 3D modeling apps to expensive laser scanners to kite photography to drones will be discussed. What is the right tool for the job? How easy is it really? How much can you expect to spend? What types of sites are best for each method?